Explorations Beyond Reality
Living Evolution
Through
Genetic Memory

By Shelley Kaehr, Ph.D.

Also by Shelley Kaehr, Ph.D.
Books
Beyond Reality: Evidence of Parallel Universes
Lifestream: Journey into Past & Future Lives
Gemstone Journeys
Galactic Healing
Origins of Huna: Secret Behind the Secret Science
Edgar Cayce's Guide to Gemstones, Minerals, Metals & More
Divinaton of God: Anceitn Tool of Prophecy Revealed
Lemurian Seeds: Hope for Humanity
Just Write It! Step By Step Guide to Writing & Publishing Your First Book
With This Ring: Making the Ultimate Commitment To Yourself

Guided Meditation audio CD's
Lifestream: Journey into Past & Future Lives
Journey to Grief Recovery
Origins of Huna: Ho'oponopono Cord Cutting
Journey to Spirit: Meeting Your Guides
Journey to Spirit: Attracting Abundance
Galactic Healing: The Elements Within You

Videos & Training Programs
Galactic Healing
Gemstone Journeys: Laying-on-of-Stones
Stones of Power

Books & CD's available at:
www.galactichealing.org

Explorations Beyond Reality
Living Evolution
Through
Genetic Memory

By Shelley Kaehr, Ph.D.

FIRST EDITION
First Printing, 2006

Cover design by Shelley Kaehr
Slit experiment graphic by Phil Laird
Cover photo NASA

Library of Congress Control Number: 2006934092
Kaehr, Shelley A., 1967--
                    Explorations beyond reality: living evolution
through genetic memory /
Shelley Kaehr—1ˢᵗ ed.
                p.   cm.
                Includes bibliographical references.
                ISBN 0-9777556-8-1

Out of This World Publishing/An Out of This World® Production does not participate in, endorse, or have any authority or responsibility concerning private business transactions between our authors and the public.

All mail addressed to the author is forwarded but the publisher cannot, unless specifically instructed by the author, give out an address and phone number.

If you wish to contact the author or would like more information about this book, please write to the author in care of An Out of This World® Production and we will forward your request. Please write to:

Shelley Kaehr, Ph.D.
c/o An Out of This World® Production
P.O. Box 610943
Dallas, TX 75261-0943

Visit the author online at www.galactichealing.org
www.outofthisworldpublishing.com

Acknowledgements

Thank you to the late Joe Crosson, who initially inspired this research and to many others without whom I could never have completed this work including:

Martha Switzer, Lori Edwards, Linnea Martinson, Beverly Love, Lisa Lyon, Stephanie Smith, Jane Li, Priscilla Thompson, Will Rosasco and the wonderful listeners at Coast to Coast AM & my clients for their willingness to share their time & energy with me.

To my parents Mickey and Gail and my brother Mark, as always I could not do my work if not for you, thanks!

Table of Contents

Introduction

For the past seven years I have been working as a counselor offering journeys into past lives and possible future realities. As I reported in my earlier books, I entered this path after this type of work made such a profound improvement in my own life in helping me deal with unresolved grief, I decided to become a counselor to hopefully make some kind of impact on others.

After several years, I have worked with so many clients and have had the incredible opportunity to explore so many different states of consciousness that I actually have more questions about past life regression now than I did when I first began.

In my lectures people always ask me if I really believe that past lives are real and are sometimes shocked at my response, in which is that I do not know if any of it is real at all. The more I'm in this business, the more I doubt whether the explanation for all the things stored in the subconscious can be explained simply by the fact that we've lived before.

This book is my answer to many of the theories currently running around in my mind as to what the explanation could be for all of these otherworldly adventures we have in altered states of consciousness.

I hope it will shed some light or at least cause you to pause and consider all of the possibilities out there as we continue to understand ourselves at a higher level.

One
A Higher Power or Intelligence

I am often asked amidst all of the complexities I explore in my books whether or not I believe in a higher intelligence or God that created all of the things we experience here in our known universe.

The answer to that question is a resounding 'YES!' I happen to believe that it is possible that simultaneous lives and parallel realities are all possible within the framework of some divine creation. Where when and how it all began is certainly one of the mysteries of man, and one which I believe we will probably never be able to answer with any certainty, or at least not using the same faculties we currently use to analyze our world.

The more I delve into things, the more I become aware that we have no clue what is really going on out here. It seems every week in the news we hear about 'new developments' in science, yet a few months later, more 'new developments' will come along to totally discount all we just concluded.

Even science, as much as we have come to rely on it to solve our most pressing problems, was at some point created by man. It is part of that collective illusion we have all bought into to help us wade through the time stream, and yet some are so persistent about insisting our scientific method is the end all be all of the world and that nothing that does not fit within its walls can be credible. There are many things we are currently doing here in our society I believe will have to be ultimately overhauled in order for mankind to evolve.

Certainly within the scientific framework, new developments are always born, yet I am speaking here of the underlying philosophical beliefs held by so many people today. Gradually outmoded and stringent ways of thinking will have to dissolve so we can reach a higher plane.

Where God or Source energy fits into it all is somewhat hard to say. Is our creator sitting up in a cloud smiling, or more often I would imagine, frowning at the foibles of his earthly children? Or is our God more of a force, a divine light or spark, that lovingly allows us to create our highest vision while simultaneously destroying ourselves? There is no way at present to fully know the answers to these questions except through our own unique belief systems and faith.

The more I work with people and live in this world, the more I am convinced that all suffering here in the physical plane is caused by the way we view reality. It is easy to get inside ourselves and change the way we see things and immediately our entire world is new.

I would like to see all suffering end and a higher understanding of our own power become a permanent fixture in our consciousness.

Two things are infinite – the universe and human stupidity; and I'm not sure about the universe.

– **Albert Einstein**

PART ONE
PARALLEL UNIVERSES

Two
More Science to Support the Strangeness

Since writing *Beyond Reality*, I have come to a higher understanding of the science that supports some of the cutting edge theories we are considering today about the nature of our known universe and I would like to summarize some of these here.

When you think of how far we've come in such a short period of time, it really is quite baffling. My parents still revel in the fact we have indoor plumbing and air conditoning these days, but we've come so much further than that. We're now duplicating ourselves, exploring the boundaries of our known universe and changing our definitions of our world practically on a daily basis.

Even our old tried and true friend planet Pluto has lost its status amongst the other heavenly bodies we relate to as it recently became dwarfed. I'm sure there are lots of unhappy astrologers thanks to that decision!

The point is that we are not living in a stagnant world. We are in a state of constant flux.

I believe even in the 'good ol'days' in the earlier part of the twentieth century that we were also in that same state of flux, but lately things are accelerating at lighting speed. It is very challenging to be on planet earth at this time amidst so much change, and yet it is exhilerating.

With those changes,I think it is always important to take a quick look back to remind ourselves of just how far we've come.

I offer this section up as a left-brained approach to lay the foundation for some of the things we are going to explore in the book so that those theories will have a deeper meaning and higher understanding.

Three
Scientific History in a Nutshell

Our ideas of modern science began in 1665 when Sir Isaac Newton discovered the force of gravity after he was inadvertently hit on the head by a falling apple.

Later, in 1801, an experiment was conducted that is critical to our thinking today called the Double Slit Experiment. Sir Thomas Young (1773-1829) passed a beam of light through two slits and based on the unpredictable way it behaved, concluded that light can function as both wave and particle simultaneously.

In 1927, the Heisenberg Uncertainty Paper was presented by Wilhelm Heisenberg. This theory says that: "the more precisely the position is determined, the less precisely the momentum is known in this instant and vice versa."

I mentioned this in my last book, but what does it really mean? If you look at the picture of the truck in the photo on the next page, how fast is it moving, in your opinion, based on seeing it in the picture?

The Heisenberg Uncertainty Principle is talking about momentum, or the mass, or size of an object multiplied by its velocity or speed. If I look at the truck and see it at a particular place on the street in one moment, that cannot guarantee how fast it is actually moving and the more locked in I am to only considering the location facts, the less likely I am to actually figure out the speed. There is no certainty in that instant of how fast this truck is moving. It is a total unknown.

Why these two theories are paramount to our understanding of parallel universes and quantum physics in general is because the combination of these two experiments gives evidence of parallel universes.

If you pass that particle of light through the slits as Sir Thomas did, what he found was that sometimes the particle of light went through the slot on the right, sometimes it went through the slot on the left, but sometimes, in totally unpredictable ways, the particle of light went through both slots at once. Therefore if a light particle can act wavelike and be in two places at once, and that light is made up of the same stuff you and I and everything else in the known universe is made up of, then why can't you and I also be in two places at once?

This 'proves,' as much as possible at this

Can You Tell How Fast This Truck is Moving?

The Heisenberg Uncertainty Paper says you cannot simply by looking because it is in flux.

Double Slit Experiment

When a light particle was passed through the board with the slits, it behaved randomly and sometimesthe particle was in two places at once which means parallel universes may be real!

point, anyhow, that the possibility of parallel realities is reality and not fiction.

Later this theory was put on paper by Hugh Everett III in the Many Worlds Theory of 1957 which states: "whenever several viable possibilities exist, the world splits into many worlds – one for each possibility."

And in 1960 the term 'universe' which literally translates into 'one world' was corrected by Andy Nimmo who coined the term 'multiverse,' which is: "An apparent universe, a multiplicity of which go to make up the whole universe."

Four
Blue Mountain

The latest developments in multiple universes seem to parallel the invention of a new supercomputer called Blue Mountain which is housed in Los Alamos, New Mexico.

This incredible machine is able to simultaneously process 6,144 computations at once – a feat once thought impossible – and is opening the doors to lots of new possibilities in the wacky world of quantum events by proving that a single particle can occupy two places at once.

The computer you have at home has two choices, it can be either on or off, which are represented by the numbers 1 and 0, respectively. The quantum computer can be set at 1 and 0 at the same time. This supercomputer will eventually be able to crack all types of codes and answer questions that should have taken mankind millions or even billions of years to answer, and nobody really understands for sure why the two states can occur simultaneously, yet at this time, this offers what I believe is the most compelling evidence yet that parallel universes actually exist. It's as if the computer can exist in two worlds at once. The only thing is the computer cannot tell us what it is like to be in those states and we have yet to understand all it has to teach us.

From what I have learned of it, it seems the machine is actually more intelligent than its makers, however, so there is no telling what the implications of such an invention will actually be. There is an old saying that no machine can fully understand itself, and in this case, I believe the machine, if it could talk to us, could probably tell us much about the unknown aspects of creation.

Is your head swimming yet? I realize this is a lot of information to process, yet I can assure you it all leads up to one thing: parallel universe as fact, not fiction. Now that the left side of the brain has been satisfied, let's begin to delve into the realm of the unexplained.

Five
Parallel Universes via Hypnosis

A lot has happened in the three years since I put out my book *Beyond Reality: Evidence of Parallel Universes*.

The whole grand experiment started for me after having a shared dream with a friend one night several years ago and since then, I have continued to explore possibilities and ask questions I still do not have certain answers to.

In order to obtain the case studies for *Beyond Reality*, I created a hypnotic process and guided clients into a space where they would discover whether or not they actually lived in parallel realities.

In that first book, I did not disclose the process, primarily because I did not want that to overshadow the message of the book – that you and I have the power to create the lives we want simply by changing our thinking and that science supports this fact.

In the years since then, I have had the amazing opportunity to travel around the world giving lectures on *Beyond Reality* and taking audiences through the process with many exciting results, so for the first time, in this book, that process is revealed so you can try it yourself at home.

After discussing the theories in the first book with so many people and taking groups through the process, I learned a lot and much occurred to me during these years that I want to share with you now through several of the most amazing case studies I ran across.

Some of the things experienced by these groups absolutely blew me away, and I'm sure you'll agree, they'll give you lots to think about.

The main thing I discovered is that parallel universes need not be visited by some man made machine taking up tons of valuable land, but can be more readily accessed within the realm of your own mind.

Next, we'll look at some of the more profound examples of this that I've run into over the past few years.

Six
The Twin Towers

The case study that stands out the most happened when I was in Austin, TX, doing a two day expo a couple of years ago. On Saturday I gave my lecture and guided the group through the process of tapping into parallel universes that you will see later in this book, and on Sunday, a young man stopped by my booth to share what happened to him during this guided journey:

"When you asked us to travel down the path into our parallel reality, I went to 2005 in New York City, only in this reality, the twin towers were still standing," he said.

This fascinated me and I asked him to give me details about what exactly was different that caused the towers to still be here verses in our own universe where they were gone. He paused and thought about this for quite awhile and could not ever give a very detailed answer:

"I don't know how to explain it," he said. "It's like there was a bit of a different attitude that allowed it. People had a bit higher level of unity, I'd say, only things in that reality still aren't perfect, and if they don't change, it could still happen."

I asked him to go home that night and to see if anything else occurred to him about this. The next day he came back and told me this:

"There was still a lot of tension in the place where I went, but it was like it had not reached a boiling point yet. Here, in our current world, it's as if we already boiled over now after this happened and some pressure has been relieved. In the parallel world, the pressure was still there, but there was a chance for it to change."

"Did it change, do you think?" I asked.

"I'm not sure," he said, "I don't think I wanted to go out from that moment to see whether or not it did. I have a feeling it didn't."

"Which reality was better – that one, or this one?" I asked.

"Neither," he said. "They are just different,

that's all. I wish I could say the other one was so much better and people treated each other better, but it's just not the case. It's just a delay in response."

"Do you think there are other places where this event never happened at all?" I asked.

"Yeah, maybe," he said, "I mean, I think that is certainly possible, but it wasn't the place where I went."

Was he referring to the higher level of tolerance and understanding we hope society rises to in the future – a place where war and turmoil are at a minimum and not the norm? That was my interpretation, although such things are quite subjective to our interpretations.

This way of thinking is what much of our modern peace movement is based on. If we can simply begin to focus on the things we want to see in the world, such as a peaceful world where war is non-existent and we all treat each other with compassion, then that will be the reality we exist in. If enough of us think this way, we can change the world.

An angel can illuminate the thought and mind of man by strengthening the power of vision.

— *St. Thomas Aquinas*

Seven
Spiritual Guidance

In my work as a hypnotherapist, I find myself dealing with people in the so called 'New Age' movement. Many people, including myself, have often referred to the intuitive guidance we receive as coming from a place outside ourselves, or from some spirit guides.

Guides, defined by most people's standards, are our angels from above who lovingly support and guide us through our reality here on earth.

Others call this aspect of the human mind the "higher self," or all knowing "over soul" who knows all that we were, are and shall be in the future.

After working for the past several years with clients and listening to hypnotic journeys of thousands of people, I view this phenomenon very differently now, particularly after hearing one amazing case study.

I was speaking at a conference and took the group through a hypnotic journey into a parallel reality (the same one you can go through in this book) and she approached me the next day to give feedback on the experience.

She said that during the process she traveled to modern day China where she was simultaneously residing in a parallel universe:

"When I went there I saw I was a woman. I was very poor and extremely sad because the government had just killed my daughter."

She was in fact, referring to the atrocious twenty-first century genocides being committed against females in mainland China.

"It really made me sad to see this," she explained. "I was still thinking about it when I went home last night so I decided to meditate and go there to see her again, to see if I could help."

"What happened then?" I asked.

"I saw her there, sitting in her nearly empty house in a chair. I floated up to her and just when I got there, she turned around and said, 'Who's there?' I said 'It's me, I'm part of you and I am here to help you!' so I held her and I noticed she seemed to feel better and calmed

down a bit. It made me feel better too."

This exchange made me perceive the concept of guides in a totally new way. What if these "guides" are actually aspects of the self, in which case, the higher self concept takes on a newly expanded definition.

I read an article in a scientific journal that suggested this very thing: that you may actually go out into your own future to bring back information to yourself so you can make better decisions.

Is it possible that the 'little voice in your head' is actually your own, a future version of yourself traveling back in time to warn you of something, or could it be the voice of the unified field of consciousness? I now believe it is something along these lines rather than a super-natural occurrence.

You may have seen the *Matrix* films and I think they are one of the best examples of much of what we are talking about now.

In each of the films, the main characters Neo and Trinity have to plug in to the matrix and go inside the illusion in order to save the world.

The spaceship driver is outside the matrix and is guiding them by talking to them. Neo cannot see the driver but he talks to him in his head and says "Turn left! Now right," or whatever direction is needed and if Neo wants his life to run more smoothly, he follows those directions.

This is a good visual for what we are talking about here. The unseen force helping you make your life a blissful peace could be you or an aspect of you living in a parallel universe. Amazing, isn't it?

In this case, the woman's account of her life in China certainly seemed to suggest that there was a higher part of herself who was able to lovingly support her Chinese counterpart.

If that's true, it suggests that the loving guidance we receive on a daily basis could also be coming from a future version of ourselves.

Eight
One Reality Ends, Another Begins

Another of the more memorable cases I heard happened to a woman who reported she was driving with her kids on the highway one night. The kids were apparently screaming in the back seat and she turned around to discipline them. Then, the unthinkable happened:

"When I turned back around, there was a semi truck coming right for us. There was nothing I could do, no time to react," she said.

Then a miracle happened:

"The next thing I knew I was still driving, but now I was on the other side of the road headed in the opposite direction. The truck was no-where to be found, the kids were still screaming and when I looked at the clock, nearly twenty minutes had passed."

Did a guardian angel step in to save the day? Certainly that is one possibility. Another could be that her consciousness shifted into another reality as the previous one ended.

If it's true that multiple worlds coexist, then it is possible that when her life in one reality came to an end that she just picked up in another.

This would bring interesting implications to the discussion of death. We've heard our whole lives that there is no death of the spirit, that we shall go on from here, but if all worlds and lives exist at once, that takes the concept of life after life to a whole new level.

Nine
Passing through solid objects

We've heard that everything around us is illusion – that solid objects only appear that way because of a density of molecules and we've seen on science fiction shows how characters seem to defy all logic by passing through solid walls, but does this really happen in the real world?

Another client told me about this incredible miracle:

"My friend and I were on our way home from work in the 5:00 p.m. rush hour. There were three lanes of traffic, all full and moving along rapidly. Two lanes went straight ahead and the right lane turned right. We were in the center lane but we wanted to turn right. However there was a car directly to my right as I sat in the passenger seat. We turned right anyway and that car went ahead of us in

the center lane! The driver said, "Did you see that???" I said "Yes," and we drove home in complete awe.
To all appearances that car went through us!"

I certainly believe this is possible. In the next chapters we'll look at this further.

Ten
Missing Objects

Have you ever wondered about certain objects that go missing and you are certain you put them in a specific place?

I was on a radio show recently and the host said he did an entire show on this phenomenon. I used to joke around that my keys were always slipping through a tear in the space fabric, only to reappear again at some unknown moment in the future.

What's strange is when I know for certain I put the object in an exact spot, it is gone, and then days later when I look again, there it is. I'm sure something like this has probably happened to you. Could it be possible that you are temporarily stepping into another universe where things are almost alike yet slightly different and that when you come back into the original space, your lost object is there, right where you left it? I believe this is certainly possible.

A listener on the radio called in one night with a strange tale about a friend who went into a parallel world, picked up an object and consciously brought it back into this reality. When I first heard this story, I told the listeners I had no idea such a thing was possible – certainly it was nothing I had ever heard before, although I am always open to the fact that I believe anything is possible.

After the show, another listener wrote in with the following information:

Dear Shelley:
A caller on Coast told of returning from a parallel universe with an object taken from that universe. Your comment was that you had not heard of this before. Perhaps I could shed some light on this very real occurrence. I am a pipe carrier of the Lakota people this is not an uncommon event. I have been shown things by spirit helpers and had these things manifested in this reality. Also during the ghost dance, people have been known to return from the land of the grand fathers with star material clinched in their fists."

I wanted to get further clarity and received this response:

"The people who danced the ghost dance visited their dead relatives. The objects that

they brought back with them were said to be gifts given to them from long dead relatives to be taken back with them.

And when they woke up from a coma like state they held various objects tightly in their fist. While others held star food given to them by star people, this has never been revealed to me. Now you have to wonder if death as we know it is merely an actual movement to another dimension. I hope this will help you better understand what I first wrote to you about."

Much of this writer's information stems from the Lakota creation myth and the belief that the tribe originated from the stars.

"I've been on a calendar, but I've never been on time."
                    – Marilyn Monroe

Eleven
Looking Back and Forth in Time

The question is how to shift our attention from reality to reality. Is it actually possible to do this, and if so, what happens when we do? And could we really bring objects from one space to another? One man wrote in to tell me how time seemed to replay itself on three different occasions:

"I'm a Christian and I believe in God and that when I die, I will go to Heaven. But I also know that there are things in this world that just can't be explained, or, that we don't want to understand. Anyway, there have been three different times in my life that very strange things have happened to me that I just can not explain. The first was back in the 90s, I was at a club having dinner and just for grins, I decided to buy a cigar. The person came by and gave me the 'cigar menu' for me to look over. I was looking

*at the menu and noticed a funny name for one of
the cigars. It was called 'The Fighting Cock',
like what you would call a rooster. Well, I just
laughed and decided to order that one. Now,
the menu was always right in front of me at all
times and I had never been to that club or any of
it's 'sister' clubs ever so that was the first time I
ever saw the menu or any of the names of the
cigars. When the person came back to ask what
cigar I wanted, I grinned and said laughing,
"I'll have the one called The Fighting Cock".
He just looked at me and said "I'm sorry, we
haven't had that one for over a year". I said
back to him "But it's right there on the menu"
and Shelley, when I turned and looked at the
menu, it wasn't there. I looked up and down the
menu and it was as if it was never there. But I
swear I saw it when I first looked at the menu.
There was no way anyone could have switched
the menu for another one and I'd never been to
any of the other clubs that used to sell it. The
waiter looked puzzled but not near as puzzled as
I was. How was it that I was able to see the
name of a cigar on their menu that they used to
sell but didn't any more and then not see it
again when I looked a second time? It was
almost as if I was looking at a menu that existed
in the past but not the present. Like I was
looking back in time in a way. It was very weird
and made me wonder about it for days.*

The second time something like that

*happened was after I moved to San Antonio. I
was sitting on my bed and suddenly the little red
light on my caller ID started flashing like it does
anytime a call comes in. I looked over at it but
wondered why the phone wasn't ringing. What
had made the red light start flashing? Then I
looked at the name on the Caller ID and it was
my girlfriend at the time and the time on the
Caller ID was 1:10 p.m. but the actual time was
12:55 when it started flashing. I thought it was
odd. Then, the very second it became 1:10 pm,
the phone rang and it was my girlfriend calling,
just like it said on my caller ID. She had called
the exact time the Caller ID said that she had
already called which was 15 minutes from the
time I saw it. Almost as if I was seeing something in the future. I freaked to say the least.*

*Then the third time something like this has
happened was last January when I was sitting in
Church. I was sitting there reading over the
bulletin that they give you when you walk into
the sanctuary that tells what songs are going to
be sung, etc. While I was looking over it, (now,
this was before the services had even started,
people were still coming in to sit down) I noticed that it said they were going to have the
Lord's Supper. It was listed during the program
as one of the events. Not as something that
would happen next week etc., but that exact
day. I thought to myself, 'that makes sense since
today is the first Sunday of the year'. Then I*

didn't think anything about it. I just thought we were going to be having the Lord's Supper on that day, no big deal. Well, I didn't look at it after that and just started listening to the morning announcements. The preacher said something like, 'I'm a Christian and I believe in God and that when I die, I will go to Heaven. But I also know that there are things in this world that just can't be explained, or, that we don't want to understand. Anyway, there have been three different times in my life that very strange things have happened to me that I just can not explain. And remember, next week we'll be having the Lord's Supper". I thought to myself, 'But, it says right here that it will be today.' Then I looked at the bulletin and it wasn't there. I looked up and down back and forth on every page and it just wasn't there anywhere to be seen. Again, it was like I was seeing something that hadn't happened yet. By this time I was really freaking out and wondering what was really going on. I started thinking about how that sort of thing had happened two times already and this time in church was a third time. Now I knew it wasn't my imagination but maybe something else but I didn't know what. I have no idea what to make of any of it but since it's happened three times already, I don't doubt it will happen again.

I would love to try to understand what is going on with me, it's almost like I'm seeing into a parallel dimension from time to time, just like ours but, oh, I don't know, I can't put my finger on it but I know it's 'something', I just don't have a clue what."

One man shared his theory of what he called 'perpendicular realities,' which could offer a possible explanation for the above scenario:

"Current physics say space is curved, therefore, if you travel in a straight line you will intersect that line several times in several places. This means several instances where you may come across yourself, or considering that neurons fire at approximately the speed of light, as the thoughts travel at that velocity they continue to slow simply because as you reach the speed of light time slows. If you intersect your own line you may have the sense of those thoughts be-fore."

The future cannot be predicted,
but futures can be invented.
                    – Dennis Gabor, 1963

Twelve
Stepping Into Another World

I received the following letter from someone who heard me on the radio:

"Dear Dr. Shelley, I have a friend in St. Petersburg, Florida that had a very unusual experience when he was ten years old. One day when he was taking a walk outside he had a several second experience to where he was walking on a board walk inside an older woman's body. I asked him what he seen. He told me there were no cars, the houses had the look of older models and there was nothing but horses and carriages.

I put a lot of thought into this and it sounds like he accidentally went into another person's body within a time period in the past and at the same time she possibly visualized things happening in the 20th century in his little ten year old body.

Sort of reminds me of when you're listening to the radio at night and the frequency of the song you're listening to merges off into another broadcast then eventually comes back."

Two things came to mind when I read this. First, it may be an example of something discussed earlier in the book. Perhaps this ten year old was a guide or somehow connected to the older woman and vise versa.

Second, about the radio frequencies, several years ago I wrote about the death of my friend in a hiking accident in New Mexico. I first told the story of his death in *Lifestream: Journeys into Past & Future Lives* and again discussed the strange coincidence of meeting a man who helped him in his final minutes on earth in *Beyond Reality*.

So many strange and unexplained things happened surrounding his death; I may spend the next several years relaying it all.

In this case, my friend had been gone for several years when I received a wedding invitation from my cousin in Albuquerque, New Mexico (my hometown) for her wedding on the 7th anniversary of my friend's death.

I found it to be an incredible coincidence, especially since I had not been back to New Mexico in quite awhile, so I made plans to attend.

My friend lived in Santa Fe at the time of his death and I decided that I would stop there on my way to pay some respects to him by dropping flowers off near his home.

I had never been to this place before and I recall driving aimlessly through the neighborhood where I thought he lived. The streets in Santa Fe are very curvy and confusing and although I could see the place on the map, I was lost.

Right when I was about to turn and give it up so as not to be late to the wedding rehearsal dinner, the song I was listening to on the radio was interrupted by a very old song that my friend used to love.

I thought I was hearing things at first, but sure enough, after two more simple turns down the side streets, I found myself in front of his old house. Immediately the song on the radio stopped and went back to what I was hearing before.

We know our loved ones are close to us, but this seemed to give extra evidence of that! They say that matter can never be destroyed, it only changes form. I think it's true!

For I dipped into the Future, far as human eye could see; saw the vision of the world, and all the wonder that would be.

– Alfred, Lord Tennyson, 1842

Thirteen
Reality of Time Travel

Is it possible for us to expand our awareness to such an extent that we could find ourselves awake and aware of past times? I believe it is. I have long said I believe we are time traveling all the time and are perhaps not aware of it.

The easiest way for me to demonstrate how we do it is to have you think for just a moment about where you'll be tomorrow during lunch. Go ahead and pause now to think about that.

Did you imagine it? Where were you? Were you at the office, eating while you worked through the lunch hour or did you go home? Did you meet friends at a local restaurant, or did you skip lunch entirely?

I would imagine you thought of something, regardless of what it was. Could you see yourself at lunch as if you were watching yourself on TV, or were you looking out your own eyes chomping down on a sandwich? Could you taste the food as it hit your mouth? Could you feel the crispy texture of the lettuce in your salad?

Regardless of how you did that, the fact is, you just time traveled! You projected yourself into a future event. If you can go to the future, you should also be able to travel into the past.

Think about your first pair of shoes. Can you see them in your mind's eye? What do they feel like? When I asked you that, I saw a visual image of some of those hard white leather shoes they used to put on babies a long time ago. Had I ever recalled that before – no, yet I was able to just then, so in essence, I just traveled back in time to 1967! I would imagine you did also, didn't you?

It would seem possible that we could also wake up and transport our entire consciousness to any time past or present where we would like to be. The trouble with this is that because we cannot see and touch these things, some say they are not real. Science values that which can be reproduced – touched and felt with our physical senses.

Perhaps someday, somehow, our definition of such things will be expanded and these experiences quantified.

Fourteen
Tree of Life

During the guided meditations, I took people to a relaxing space, which you can go to yourself in just a bit, and in that space, they were given the opportunity to notice several paths of possibility.

If it is true that every time you make a decision a new universe is created, then even the choice to turn right instead of left, in theory, could alter the fate of your entire life and change your destiny forever.

Just like a tree branches out, so do opportunities and choices. If you turn left instead of right, once you do that, you will soon be presented with another decision to make – right or left. Once you choose right, you head down a new path with new choices that are different than the ones you would have had you turned left, and so on and so on. Eventually a sort of tree of life is formed with many branches.

In the next set of case studies, I want to share what happened when people traveled from one choice to the other, going on a path of self discovery to the unknown.

In the exercise, participants were asked to notice three paths of light and travel down the brightest one, then pick between two paths and last, notice only one path.

One woman went to India first:

"I was in India for my first location. It was very busy and my purpose was that I was an actress in the year 1930. Then the two paths appeared and the brighter one led me to Japan where I lived again as a female in 1740 and I had several children and a loving husband. The next path that appeared led me to 1873 in the Western United States where I was a man."

Another woman discovered a connection with her spirituality in the present:

"The first place I went was to Sedona, AZ, in 1985 where I went in this lifetime to get back in touch with the spiritual side of life and the brightness of my life on the spiritual path. Next, I went to the Bay Area in 2005 and I saw myself reconnecting with spiritual people and beings and feeling connected. I'm glad to be here and I am enjoying the connection I feel. Last, I saw myself in a year from now in 2006 getting in

touch and making large strides in physical and spiritual healing and feeling the joy of the journey continuing, feeling very light, young, being healthy. I feel much joy and peaceful and calm."

One woman saw herself in several different realities:

"The first path led me to 1860 in the Snake River area. I saw myself by the river and saw trees all around me. I was the Native American female healer for the tribe and I saw myself performing healings. The next path led me to the 1800's in the Pacific Northwest in the San Juan Islands. I was a male and was a hunter for the tribe and part of the council. I saw myself sitting around the tribal fire at night. The last path led me to England, although I am not sure of the year. I was a male and was a messenger of some kind riding horses, dressed in tall boots and a cloak in an area of a tree grove and waterfall."

Another woman had a vivid experience of four alternative realities:

"When I went into the room it was red with chandeliers on the right side and a jungle on the left with much greenery. When I went down the first path, I was a fisherman in China on a canoe in a valley of a river with green water

and green mountains and stillness.

Next, I went to Germany and was standing there observing a church. It is tall with black still metal bells. This is in 1940.

The next path is in 1930 France and I see a man riding a horse, and the last path is in 1920 in the jungle. Everything is very lush and green and beautiful. There is a waterfall and it is quite peaceful there.

The common theme of all of these places is stillness and being present, being a witness to my surroundings, observing being alone with no others around in solitude. My purpose here is to love, to appreciate beauty and to be kind and to be peaceful just being me with all the space around me. I also got that I need to meditate for my highest good."

Another woman experienced the following:

"The first path was Caracas, Venezuela and I am living with a brother of a man and being abused. I am trapped and couldn't get out. The year is 1968. The second path is in India and I am like a nun. I feel overwhelmed by the immense need around me and not being able to make a dent in it. I am healing through nursing. The third path is in Lake Tahoe. I am a Native

*American medicine man. The fourth is Georgia.
I am a slave and healer. Work is done in the
quarters and I learn to know what it is like to be
oppressed. Despite that, I feel a connection to
all and this life time I am learning to be fully
who I am and to not allow abuse in any rela-
tionship and to allow myself to live truly."*

"This is like deja vu all over again,"

–Yogi Berra

Fifteen
Déjà vu'

That strange feeling you've been in this exact spot, having this exact conversation before may have a completely logical explanation.

Mainstream scientists try to explain it away by suggesting this happens because of the different lengths in our optic nerves. Since the eye is like a lens taking in information to the optic nerve which then sends it to the brain for interpretation, the theory says that if one optic nerve is shorter than the other, the information gets to the brain faster than it can traveling along the longer nerve, therefore, information is interpreted twice.

Nice try, but to me that sounds a bit silly. So many of our déjà vu experiences involve longer spans of time than just a few minutes, I don't believe it can simply be explained away as a problem with our eyes and brains. That would be like a doctor concluding you have a 'virus' when he or she cannot explain an illness any other way.

There are two types of déjà vu – the first is the feeling you have been in a place or met a person before although you have never seen them in this lifetime. The second is when you find yourself having an exact conversation that you know for certain you have experienced yourself having before. To me, the second kind is far stranger than the first.

For myself, I have had several profound experiences like this, as I am sure you have. Once I went as a lecturer on a cruise ship to the Caribbean and we stopped in St. Martin and St. Thomas and had the day in both places to look around and explore.

I fell instantly in love with St. Martin. The energy there, to me was fantastic and I enjoyed the shops and the nice people there. When I got to St. Thomas, though, the feeling was entirely different. It seemed more foreboding to me there and as I walked along the cobblestone streets looking up at the signs on the stores designed to make you feel like you were a 'Pirate of the Caribbean' yourself, I put my foot on one place in the sidewalk and instantly froze.

A rush of energy ran through me and I knew that my foot had walked on that exact spot before. I paused to look out off the island at the

beautiful mountainous landscape and I knew
with great certainty that I was home. I had been
here before and I probably lived in the time of
the pirates, which instantly explained why I
have a fascination with them.

Another interesting case I heard of this
kind of déjà vu came from a caller on a radio
show I was on:

*"My wife and I were planning a vacation to
Cuba and several months before I went I had a
very vivid dream about a bar in a place I had
never been before. Several months later when
we were on the trip, we went into a bar and I
couldn't believe my eyes. It was the place I had
seen in my dream. It was exactly how I had
seen it – very empty with only a few chairs in it
and the people there were the same ones I had
seen earlier. I wondered why this was so important and what it meant. I guess I still do."*

In theory we would like to believe these
experiences of déjà vu come to us for a reason,
as warnings or encouragement so it is not
surprising the man was perplexed by the significance of this foreign bar.

A friend of mine had a profound déjà vu
while we were having dinner in a restaurant one
evening.

He stopped mid sentence and looked
over to his right at the waitress taking the order
at the table next to us.

"What's wrong" I asked.

"Nothing," he said, "it's just that when I heard the voice of that waitress, I looked down at my steak and I remembered that I have seen all of this before."

"What do you mean?" I asked.

"Just a few weeks ago I saw all of this in my head. The food, the table, and I can remember hearing that girl's voice."

"What do you think it's telling you?" I asked.

"To me, it means I am right on track. I am exactly where I am supposed to be."

Déjà vu can also involve more than just seeing places – people can also come into the picture, which is what happened to one man who sees people in his mind then meets them in person later:

"When is it when Dreams become a reality? I dream in color constantly. I envision people who I never met and then suddenly I meet them in person."

That note reminded me of how I became interested in gem and mineral healing after I had a dream one night several years ago about a dark haired man. His image zoomed in like a lens on a camcorder and then faded away. Two weeks later at an event I attended in Las Vegas, there was this man who I found to be quite familiar but could not place him. That night in my hotel room I replayed the dream and realized it was the man I had seen a couple of weeks before in my dream. As it turned out, he was a Native American healer who showed me the healing properties of stones and minerals and that, of course, has played such a major role in my life, I can't imagine what would have happened had I not paid attention to that bit of divine guidance.

Perhaps all of us receive such premonitions but I think in our busy world we are often too quick to dismiss these synchronicities.

I had a very strange experience in April 2005 on my trip to Peru. I went to Cusco, the city that is the cradle of the ancient Incan Civilization and traveled by train to Machu Picchu, a most amazing trip.

After touring that area my friend and I wanted to visit Lake Titicaca, which is the highest elevated lake in the world – an extremely gorgeous place to visit.

On the trip from Lima, the capitol, to Cusco, we took a plane, but on this leg of the trip, we were encouraged to take a bus to see more of the landscape.

We left to go to the bus station and discovered that they were not running and waited for several hours before finally getting an evening bus to the destination. We were on the top floor, front seat of a double-decker bus and not too long on the trip discovered what the problem was. The people were having a strike against the government and blocked the road-ways with huge boulders and set up camp there with the intention of stopping all commerce. They were angry about new laws that were cutting into their income.

Long story short, we wound up on this road with little water and no food for a period of 26 hours. It was quite grueling and at times a bit scary! It felt like I had a front row seat to something you'd see on CNN, especially when the police arrived and began to put tear gas on the crowd. Horrible!

During all of this, I got very sleepy and decided that sleep would be the best escape from this reality in order to help get through it. During my rest, I had a very strange dream about a white cathedral with pointy spires and rusty brown trim. It was very strange looking and extremely otherworldly, although the dream was quite vivid.

Later in the night I saw a large stone figure carved like a bird, yet it was unlike any I had seen before.

When we finally rolled in to the town of Puno, gateway to the lake, it was nearly 10:00p.m.and we were famished and exhausted, to say the least. We were dropped to our hotel and got directions to the only place in town open that late where we could get something to eat and drink.

As we walked down the street and into the town square, I could not believe my eyes – there was the strange church I had seen in my dream! I wondered what it meant, and just like my friend at the restaurant, I interpreted it to mean I was on the right track somehow in spite of all the trouble getting there.

We enjoyed our stay at Lake Titicaca and ended the trip by flying back to Lima. We stayed in the south side of the city near the beach and explored the first night. As we approached the main boardwalk, again, I could not believe my eyes – there was the stone bird statue right in front of me – the one from my dream. I somehow knew everything would be okay, and it was!

How we receive this otherworldly form of communication is beyond me, yet it seems our souls are guiding us, perhaps to show us we are on the right path and give validation to our lives.

Sixteen
Why You Can't Speak to Your Doppleganger

The next topic of major discussion over the past couple of years is about the previously fictionalized notion of doppelgangers. These are the carbon copies of you and me who are supposedly currently residing in our world, and who, on occasion, we may actually run into. Although we've all heard of the concept in our favorite sci-fi shows over the past several years, we're only now realizing those fictionalized accounts may be more realistic than previously imagined.

In the *Beyond Reality* book, I reported on a woman who said she and her husband were eating dinner in a restaurant and she saw her and her husband eating on the other side of the restaurant. Seems like stuff Rod Serling would have used as inspiration for an episode of Twilight Zone, but in this case, it really happened.

I wondered aloud many times what would happen if we were to speak to our doppelgangers and was told repeatedly why that would not be a good thing.

This phenomenon was explained more fully to me by a woman who was a member of the Lakota tribe. I met her in Rapid City, South Dakota, when I was up there doing a workshop about parallel universes.

She told me that in Native American tradition, it was considered to be extremely unlucky for a person to run into his or her double and if they ever did they should never speak to them, or they would be destroyed.

This superstition can be explained by science because two identical pieces of matter cannot occupy the same space or they will instantaneously disintegrate. This concept was summarized by one man who heard me on the radio and wrote in with this note:

"If a particle, (which searches endlessly for its antiparticle) through untold dimensions, ever collides with it, they will both be destroyed spectacularly i.e.; all particles have an antiparticle so, if I see, then touch my anti-self, BOOM!!"

Another woman told me a story of meeting herself, right in her own home:

"I saw my doppelganger in my kitchen once. She was in a bathrobe like one I used to wear long before and was reaching for something in the refrigerator. It startled me so I turned and went into the other room and when I tried to go back in the kitchen again, she was gone. It was really weird."

If you saw the movie *What the Bleep Do We Know!?!* you saw a similar scene with Marlee Matlin in a movie theater where one version of her walks by and moments later, another carbon copy of herself walks by.

Is that possible? I think it is!

A man wrote to tell me about a case of mistaken identity:

"I was in Kosovo doing some bodyguard work for the OSCE. I had a German man approach me and he exclaimed, "Hans! How have you been? I have not seen you for months". I have never met this man and have never gone by the name Hans. After a moment he realized I was not Hans and then commented, "You have a twin, I could have sworn you were Hans, even looking at you now I can not tell the difference."

I had a similar experience when my aunt told me she and my uncle were vacationing in Seattle when she saw me cross the street in front of her:

"You were wearing a really wild outfit," my aunt said, "and when I called out for you, you never saw us. You wouldn't even turn around."

After consulting the time period, I had a tough time convincing her I was not there and this was not me. She was completely convinced she saw me there. Strangely, the only explanation I could offer is that some years ago I moved to Seattle briefly so perhaps my doppelganger is still there and happened to cross paths with my aunt and uncle.

I'm sure you may have had a similar experience at some time in your life where someone insists they saw your twin someplace. It seems to be a fairly common occurrence. What it means, though, is hard to tell with any degree of certainty.

Seventeen
Journey Into Parallel Universes

Next you'll get to experience the journey to discover your own parallel universes.

For the exercises, the best way to do them is to get a tape player and record this in your own voice and play it back to yourself. As I have mentioned earlier, your mind loves to hear your voice.

If you don't have a recorder, you could just read it over once, then go back with your eyes closed and recreate what you read in your mind, or your third option would be to pick up a copy of this exercise I recorded for you which you can find on my website at:

www.galactichealing.org

Any way you want to do it is just fine! So get ready and let's go on this amazing inner journey.

Exercise

Go ahead and find a comfortable spot to sit and make sure you are warm enough, or cool enough and feeling comfortable and relaxed.

I would prefer you sit up for this so you will be awake enough for the process to remember what you experienced there.

Sitting in that comfortable spot, go ahead and begin to relax, however it is that you do that, by closing your eyes. Good. Now I want you to go ahead and take a deep breath in through your nose, and exhale out your mouth. And take another deep breath in through your nose – breathing in relaxation and exhaling tension and concerns. Very good.

Go ahead and imagine there's a beam of pure white light coming down in through the top of your head. Imagine the light coming in through your forehead, down into your eyes, your nose, your mouth, your jaw, and feel it moving down, down, down, through your neck, into your shoulders, into your arms, your elbows, your wrists, hands, fingertips.

Imagine this light is relaxing you and carrying away any tension and concerns you feel as it moves down through your neck and down, down, down through your shoulder blades, into your heart, into your stomach and down, down, down, into your lungs, and all the way down into the base of your spine.

Feel the light moving into your legs, into

your thighs, your knees, your ankles, your heels and into your toes. Imagine the light is like a waterfall just pouring through you, carrying away all the tension from the day and taking it down, down, down into the soles of your feet and down, down, down, into the core of the earth. Just let it all go.

Imagine the light becomes stronger now and it begins to pour out your heart, creating a golden ball of light that surrounds you by about three feet in all directions. Feel yourself floating inside this golden ball of light, safe and secure, not a care in the world, just knowing that inside this golden ball of light, only that which is of your highest good can come through. Very good!

Now I want you to imagine a beautiful angel is floating down in front of you. You can either see the angel, feel the presence of this angelic being, or just know the angel is there. Imagine the angel is a guide to you who knows every single thing there is to know about you, your soul, your soul's journey, and imagine the angel is reaching out to you now and handing you a key. So take the key and know that this key will unlock all of the things you've come here today to see, feel and experience. Very good!

Now imagine you can take the angel by the hand and the two of you will begin now to float. And you feel yourself lifting up, up, up, off of the ground, floating higher, and higher and higher. Very good.

*And as you float up, up, up, you notice
that the higher up you float, the more relaxed
you feel. Higher and higher and higher – up,
up, up. Very good!*

*Now I want you to imagine you have
floated so high in the sky you notice a doorway
in front of you. So float up to that door and
imagine you can walk through the doorway now
and find yourself inside a beautiful room filled
with very white peaceful light. This light has a
very high frequency and it immediately fills you
with a peaceful feeling. This peaceful feeling is
so powerful you instantly become twice as
relaxed as you were before you arrived and
more relaxed than you have ever been before.
Very good!*

*As you begin to look around the room
and fill yourself with this peaceful light, you
notice a doorway on the other side of the room
and that doorway is opening now and out walks
the most beautiful being you have ever seen.
This light filled presence moves slowly toward
you and you notice the being is filled with love
and light and the knowingness of the entire
universe. This omnipotent presence represent
the all that is, the cosmic awareness of everything in the entire universe is embodied within
this amazing being. And because of that, you
realize the Being knows every single thing there
is to know about you and your soul and your
soul's journey.*

And as you bathe in the unconditional love and the beautiful feelings the Being has for you, you realize you have come here today to ask this special being a very important question, and that question is this: Am I currently living in parallel universes or alternative realities, yes or no?

And you notice the first answer that pops into your mind. Very good!

And if so, how many? And you notice the first number that pops into your mind. Very good!

Now I want you to imagine the Being steps aside and three paths of light appear directly behind the Being. Very good! Imagine now you can notice which of the three paths looks or feels the lightest or brightest. Good! So imagine you can walk or float over to the lightest or brightest path now. This path repre- sents the road into a parallel universe where you currently reside. In a moment, when I count to three, you will step on the path and be trans- ferred to this alternative reality. The path is just like a moving walkway so it goes very, very quickly. Ready?

One, two, three, step on the path and feel yourself moving very quickly – zip, zip, zip, moving very quickly out, out, out, and by the time I count to three you will be there. One, floating out, out, out, Two, further and further, and Three, you're there. And you feel yourself stopping and you can be there now, so look around and notice what you see or feel.

What year is this, the first thing that comes to your mind? And where are you in the world, or are you in the world at all? Notice the first thing that comes to your mind. Very good!

How do you feel? Imagine you can look down at your feet and notice what kind of shoes you're wearing, or what kind does it feel like you're wearing? Good!

As you experience your soul in this space, what is your purpose there, or what is your reason for being? Imagine you can notice the first thing that comes to your mind.

And how does this mission, or purpose, relate to the life you're currently living? Imagine you can easily notice this. Very good!

Now imagine you can turn around and notice the path of light again. In just a moment you will step on that path and go back where you came from. Ready? One, two three, step on the path and go back, back, back and arrive back in the room where you started.

Be there now and imagine you are once again with the beautiful being of light. Imagine walking or floating up to this loving being once again and feel the love and high regard the being has for you.

Imagine now that in the presence of such high level intelligence you have the unique opportunity now to ask this Being about things you have always wondered about and you can ask these things now.

You may want to know what is the meaning of life? What is the secret of the universe? Why are we here? Take a moment to get answers to any question you may have.

Very good! Now imagine you can thank the Being and notice the Being walks back through the door where it came from. Once again you are in the room of peaceful light and you turn your attention back to your angelic guide. Take your angel by the hand and begin to walk or float back toward the door.

Open the door and you find yourself out in the clouds once again. Take your angel's hand and feel yourself floating down, down, down, back through the clouds and down, down, down, feeling the forces of gravity pulling you back to the earth until once again, you land, back where you started. Very good!

You are still surrounded by a golden ball of light, knowing that within the golden ball only that which is of highest good can come through. Imagine you can take all of the energy you need to feel awake and refreshed, but that any excess energy will begin now to float down, down, down, through your legs and out the soles of your feet going into the earth. Imagine you are sending this excess healing energy into the earth and you are now grounded, centered and balanced. Very good!

And in a moment when I count to five you will come back feeling awake, refreshed, and better than you did before. Five, grounded, centered and balanced, four, continuing to process this information in your dream state so by tomorrow morning you will be fully integrated into this new awareness, three, driving safely and being safe in all activities, two, grounded, centered and balanced, and one, you're back!

*****

So how do you feel? How was your journey? Interesting, wasn't it?

You may want to get a piece of paper out or a journal to record your experience.

PART TWO
PAST, PRESENT & FUTURE

Each has his past shut in him like the leaves of a book known to him by heart and his friends can only read the title.
~Virginia Woolf

Eighteen
The Past

For several years, I have worked as a specialist in the field of past-life regression and since my earliest childhood recollections I have always believed that we have lived before and that we will go on from here, and although my thoughts on how all that is possible has expanded through the years, I believe it is definitely among the best ways to explain certain unknown phenomenon.

One of the main ways I work with people is by helping them identify their soul purpose or reason for being. Often past life regression can be very revealing to people as they work at discovering more about themselves.

One man discovered the core of his strength in his current life:

"I am a small child in the early 1000's or late

900's," he said.

"Where are you?" I asked.

"Somewhere in Europe."

"Are you a boy or girl?"

"I am a boy and I am with my parents," he said. "As you experience the energy of your parents there, are they anyone you know in your current life?" I asked.

"Yes, they are my parents now," he said.

"Good, so what's going on there?"

"I am very sick. I've caught some kind of disease. I'm coughing and I have a fever," he said.

"Are your parents helping you?"

"Yes, but there's nothing they can do," he said. "I die."

"So what lessons did you learn from this life in the 1000's and how is this affecting your current reality?" I asked.

"The lesson is that I have to be stronger," he laughed, "and now I know why I decided to be

*so strong in this life. I cannot be stopped.
Physically I am very strong in this life. And my
parents loved me then and they love me now
too."*

People also seek past life regression to
better understand their relationships. One man
wanted to know how he knew his current girlfriend:

*"It's in the open frontier," he said. "I'm run-
ning down a trail to my cabin and I expect to
find my wife there. She is my wife," he said,
referring to the girlfriend. "and we love each
other very much and we are very happy. I can
see the smoke coming out of the chimney from
the tree tops and I know I'm close to home."*

*"Imagine you can fast forward to another
significant event in this life," I said.*

*"I see everyone crowded around a bed. My wife
is there with my friends. I am lying in the bed
and I'm dying. Why do I have to die? I can't
understand it. I'm still in my buckskin jacket
holding my rifle. I have spotted fever. My wife
sits next to me and tells me it's okay to let go
and I think if I let go of my rifle I will die for
sure. My wife tells me again it's okay and to
just let go. I take the rifle and I kiss her
goodbye and I die. I feel terrible like I let her
down and cheated her, robbed her and wasn't*

there for her. She couldn't count on me. I die and I see myself floating above my body. I look peaceful. The last thing I saw was her smiling face telling me it would be okay," he said, tears streaming from his face.

"What lessons did you learn in this life?" I asked.

"True love is everlasting."

I believe when we are young we are able to be more open to the Truth, whatever that is. Truth is in the eyes of the beholder, and yet, the purity in which children see our world is something we must observe and attempt to awaken in ourselves.

Nineteen
Children Remember

It is quite possible that we are coming back over and over again and evidence for that comes most clearly from our children who are often born knowing or somehow remembering where they most recently came from.

My friend's daughter is only five years old and within the past couple of years has started telling her mother about things she used to experience in the past.

From the moment she opened her eyes in this life, she has always wanted to have her hair perfectly done, her clothes have to be pink and frilly and she is ever concerned about all aspects of her appearance which is completely contrary to the way she was raised.

One day when she was about three, she came in and told her mother that someday they would be moving to New York City - a place her mother had never mentioned to her.

"Why do you want to do that, honey?" her mother asked.

"I just have to get back there," she said.

"How do you know about that?" her mother asked.

"Oh, I don't know," the little girl said, "my mind just goes way back."

On another day, she took her daughter to the office and she started telling everyone that God *recycles* people. The word 'recycles' was never in her vocabulary so her mother questioned her about this also, asking how she knew that. She basically told her mother that was just the way things were, as if her mother should know it.

Another client told me a similar story about his granddaughter:

"My daughter was playing with my grand-daughter one day when she looked up all of a sudden and said 'I had a daughter,' and my daughter asked her, 'Oh really, what was her name?' She got a strange far away look on her face and just dropped the subject altogether."

Another woman who has a son diagnosed with ADHD (more on that later in the book) told me about her son's apparent past life recall:

"I went to a psychic clairvoyant who had tapped into some of his past lives and said he had been a female clairvoyant in the 12th century, and saw his/her husbands death and didn't do anything to prevent it, and was angry at himself, so all lives after that he was always not wanting to "see," In World War One he was responsible for his troops dying, and then in Vietnam, the same thing happened, only a little worse because he didn't listen to orders and was responsible again for his troops death, one being his best friend he watched die, then he himself was shot in the back(he has a birth mark there) and was paralyzed and went into a catatonic state, which made sense because the year before last we thought he was having seizures, so we took him to the hospital for tests, but the MRI showed nothing, and she has said he was recalling cellular memories of that and at that time he was drawing pictures of Vietnam (although he didn't know what it was) and showing those scenes the clairvoyant talked about.

Also, when he was four years old, he got in trouble and when I put him in time out he yelled at me and said that I had been his mom 11 times, and he was mad at me and said he would never pick me for a mom again."

These are but a few of literally thousands

of such cases in existence, which to me, support the theory that past lives do exist because of the credibility of the source.

Children with no preconceived notions of such things who are instantly reporting on things they have no prior experience of are in my mind, quite reliable sources for such information.

Twenty
Spontaneous Past Life Recall

The phenomenon of remembering one's past lives is not confined to the very young. I've worked with several adults who came to me after having dreams where they were living in strange lands and recalling things they assumed to be from a past life experience.

One man vividly recalled his death:

"I remember dying in my past life. I died in a freak accident in the late 19th century in a wagon wheel when it over a ravine. After that came darkness. Moments later, I emerged from darkness into light, and LALA I'm here living in California. I was born in 1966 in San Francisco."

One client wrote me a letter describing her vivid memories of times long ago:

"Speaking in linear terms, I didn't begin to

*recall past life memories until I was around 34
years old, however most of my life I've been
plagued by not being able to remember them. It
was as if I'd left myself a note not to forget, and
I couldn't remember what it was I was supposed
to remember, I only knew I was forgetting. It
tried regressing myself, or having psychic
readings, but never got anything that I would
consider valid until I started "remembering"
things myself.*

*I remember being 7 or 8 years old and remem-
bering living in a place/time (same thing, really)
where there "was" no time. I can remember it
so specifically that's its hard even to describe.
Every once in a while "out there" premises will
come up, or I'll read about, and I have no
trouble understanding them or believing them.
There's also stuff I have to ponder then eventually conclude is garbage, so I have to go with
my feelings if I think I'm remembering something, learning it, or discarding it.*

*I've had visions, little scenes, pop into my head
during waking hours that seem unexplainable.
Usually it's either an action or else a scene as if
seeing it through someone's eyes. None of it
usually seems relevant or important.*

*Sometimes I'll read about something that seems
familiar, such as a scientific theory or religious
belief, then sometimes I'll have a vision or*

dream about how it relates to me in a past life.

These dreams or visions seem easy to identify when they're past life things or just dreams or ideas. I can't explain how, you just know. Have you ever gone back to a place you visited as a kid but haven't seen in 20-30 years? It looks the same, and you know you were there although you can't imagine yourself being there in the body you're in this minute so it seems kind of surreal. That's EXACTLY how it feels. You just "know".

One of my clearest visions came when I was drawing a bath, and the water was running in the tub. Why, I don't know. It was clear, and a painful memory. If I 'try' too hard to remember something I usually can't. They just come. I have had limited success in remembering through regression, although I have had a few visions of other lives besides that one.

How do I know this? I just know. That's another way the info comes. I literally wake up knowing it, or else it gets dumped into my head like a 20 volume book. When that happens, I have to sort through the info in my head as quickly as possible before I forget it. Sometimes I'll have to go to bed to do it; it's kind of a heavy thing when it happens. I can either ignore it, sort it out, or go crazy. Those are pretty much the choices.

For people who have past life memories, there are downsides to remembering, like horrible loneliness or longing for what you've remembered, or things that don't make sense on this plane that you need to reckon with.

For people who are pursuing past life memories I advise caution, but there may be a reason other people need to remember too. What I've remembered didn't just aid me this lifetime, it was pertinent to how I live my life now that I "know my purpose", so to speak. I believe I was programmed to remember, that I set up reminders for myself in this life to help me remember info I left for myself. But the language of the other side isn't English or even verbal, and it's hard for most people to comprehend. Some people may feel they need to know but never recognize the clues they're getting, or be able to handle the info. I'd estimate one in 10 remembers their past lives, and only a % of them chooses to work with those memories or can handle getting more than one or two."

This woman brings up some important points, mainly that the unconscious mind will only bring things up that you can handle, or on a need-to-know basis. In this case, the dreams, feelings and visions she had, as she herself recognized, were helpful to her in living a more fulfilling life in the present.

Twenty One
Animals

I'm always asked if I believe it's possible for us to have previous lives as animals and I can certainly say I've regressed several people who have vivid recollections of their lives as members of the animal kingdom.

One woman said she was a dolphin in Atlantis:

"It's very peaceful here," she said, "I just swim all day and spend time with my family. There are humans around who sometimes offer food to us and they are very kind. It is a peaceful life."

Another woman told me she was a horse in her past life. I normally like to ask people to tell me how they're feeling in the experience and in this case, I got quite a surprise:

"Trees," she said, "I see trees, and apples.

Mmmmm, they taste so good!"

"What's happening next?" I asked.

"Trees, the trees...and the apples."

I kept waiting and trying to get more of a description here and finally realized the woman was hypnotized so deeply she had actually lost some of her vocabulary temporarily and could only relate to how happy she was eating apples and looking at the landscape!

Another man who had memories of his life as a horse had more vivid details to share:

"I was a horse in a South Carolina farm. This 20 year span ran from 1803 to 1823. My owner was a deputy sheriff during that life. My master was really nice to me - didn't just treat me like an animal but a loving living thing.

The owner made sure I was staying fed and getting plenty of water to drink even during the severe drought. All the water saved in the cellar from heavy snow packed run off during previous winters was plenty to last for years. My owner did a great job conserving and boiling it, not just for himself but for me also.

During the drought which lasted for an estimate of several years. There was food to eat but very little. At least I had just enough food and water

*to keep me alive. But, food was so scarce I lost
a great deal of weight during that several year
period.*

*Every time we'd cross the train tracks cutting
through the town, my master stopped, looked
and listened. If my owner heard or saw a train
coming no matter how slow, fast, far, or close it
may seem. We made sure we didn't cross until
the train passed unless it was stopped.*

*I was a lady horse by the way. As a horse, I was
more than just a pet to my owner. I was like a
daughter to him. As a pet, I always looked up
and cherished my owner a great deal."*

Other animals I've seen in my years as a
regression therapist include wolves, bears, dogs
and cats. I'm not sure if we are really capable of
changing forms, but I do believe it is possible.
Or another explanation could be at hand – we
may just be able to tap into the consciousness of
these other creatures and notice how their lives
parallel our own.

The pet psychics who have become so
popular these days give evidence of that. You
may wonder how they are able to tap into the
feelings and thoughts of animals, yet there are
hundreds of documented cases of the miraculous
healings that occur when someone makes a
strong effort to understand their feelings.
I am occasionally called out to do animal

healings, which can be extremely interesting. Usually, for some reason, I am primarily called out to see horses and dogs, even though I am a cat owner myself.

I will never forget the very first time, several years ago, when I went to see my first horse. The owner was a woman who I had known for many years and she told me her horse was acting strange and would hardly eat at all for the past week. She was desperate to help him and asked if I could go out to give him some energy.

I wondered if it was possible at the time and told her I would be willing to experiment with it. She did not give me any background on him and to my amazement, when I went to see him; I quieted my mind and began to have thoughts occur to me about him traveling to another town and how unhappy he was about it.

When I asked my friend about it she confirmed he had recently returned from a trip to the trainers which happened to be several hundred miles away from the Dallas area. She also said she had plans to take him back up there within the month and needed him well before he could leave.

It turned out to be a compromise of sorts where he wanted her to make some special provisions for him and I told her to go to the stable and talk to him about it and when she did, his appetite returned and all was well!

This experience and many others I've

had lead me to believe there is a realm of consciousness we can all tap into if we choose. It's only a matter of quieting the mind and experiencing stillness.

Another time I was called out to a kennel where an unhappy dog seemed to be knocking on death's door.

Again, I quieted my mind and noticed how unhappy he was that his masters left him there, in a little cell, on a concrete floor, instead of having their friend come into their home to care for him.

I know they thought that they were doing what was best for him, but his health deteriorated so rapidly, they were in a panic and called me from their overseas vacation to see what could be done for him.

I told the owners that he wanted their neighbor to come get him and within hours he was good as new.

Some of this seems like common sense to me. It is something we can all do by simply getting calm and quiet and listening to the inner voice.

Our pets have incredible consciousness and intelligence and they communicate with us constantly.

There is much to be learned from the animal kingdom, that's for sure!

Listen and you will hear what I'm taking about!

Mirror, mirror on the wall, who's the fairest of them all?

–From *Snow White*

Twenty Two
Mirror, Mirror

Another way people spontaneously recall past life situations is by looking into a mirror. You may have heard about this before, but I want to briefly cover it here because it is really amazing to try, if you haven't already.

Have you ever looked at those dotted images in the cartoon section of your local Sunday newspaper where you hold the colored dots up to your face, pull the paper back and a Technicolor 3-D image appears before your eyes?

For years I tried to do this and was continually unsuccessful. Finally I somehow realized the key of it is to stare through the paper and not at it and somehow this puts the mind into that alpha trance state and the image just pops out.

Similarly, there is an exercise you can try to visually experience your past incarnations. Here's how you do it:

> 1) Go into a bathroom, preferably one with no outside windows.
>
> 2) Make sure the room is darkened with only a small backlight from under the door or a night light.
>
> 3) Stare at yourself in the mirror
>
> 4) Look either into your own eyes or at the bridge of your nose
>
> 5) Slowly begin to defocus your eyes so you look 'beyond' the mirror
>
> 6) Hold still, keep your gaze steady and your eyes open without blinking for as long as you can
>
> 7) Notice what you start to see

What you will often find, as I did, is that several images or faces begin to appear within yours. When I tried it, the faces shifted very quickly, one after another. It was quite amazing and a bit startling!

At first when you see it, you will be tempted to say 'Wow! I can't believe it!' and by doing so, you will immediately pull yourself out of the trance state you created to see it and may have to start again.

Try it and see what happens. I believe with practice you will find this process quite revealing!

When I mentioned this on a radio program one night, a woman wrote to tell me she had experienced this herself:

"I have had experiences of seeing a different self in reflections of mirrors along with the one of my physical self. This has been happening for good part of my life. After the image is seen, there are major changes that take place in my life. I had just opened up to discuss this occurrence with a friend, because the need to understand it has come to my attention. Thank you so much for shedding light of its reality. I feel better knowing I'm not alone."

Change in all things is sweet.
                                    –Aristotle

Twenty Three
Change the Past,
Change Everything

I remember when I first began taking people into past lives and I realized that sometimes people encountered very unpleasant things there. It was then that I first began the work of helping clients reinvent, or reshape reality. When there was pain, I had them imagine it was gone, or imagine the events never happened at all.

I recall discussing this with a colleague one day who told me that was unacceptable.

"You can't do that!" he said.

"Do what?" I asked.

"You can't change the reality like that. You will change history!"

This leads into the age old sci-fi conundrum where I imagine what if my grandfather was never born and if so how could I be here at all? Or likewise, if I go to the past and change things, won't that change everything and how can that be a good thing.

To me, because I do believe all possibilities are existing on different planes of existence, it makes sense to me that if I change and alter one reality, or step into a new brighter one, that it only assists me in the now and does not actually change anything other than to shift my current awareness to a place where things are running more smoothly for me.

The bottom line to me about regression therapy is whether or not it is helpful and allows the recipient to feel better in their now, at least the now they are aware of in the present moment.

I believe that the root of suffering is in our own interpretations of reality so the premise behind my work is to help you and others recreate your view of reality so it is the best it can be and your life can be the happiest and most productive possible. Happiness is the key!

Twenty Four
If past lives are real,
then what are the rules?

One of the criticisms of the theory that past lives really exist is the fact that there are no facts regarding this idea that we have lived multiple lives. Have you ever stopped to think about that? I mean, who says you are recycled and if so how many times? Why is it that you may have lived hundreds or even thousands of other lives while I may have only lived dozens? Who makes these rules anyhow?

This thought is something that I have run across over and over again when I am working with clients. I have seen people who are able to spontaneously delve into dozens of past experiences during a short hour and a half while others can't seem to get past childhood and some cannot go anywhere at all.

I always explain to people that when they are about to go into the experience of remembering 'past lives' that the process involves a recognition that the conscious mind and unconscious mind are two different things entirely.

According to modern psychology texts, your unconscious mind can only hold seven plus or minus one chunks of information at any given time. When I was in psychology class, I did not really understand what the teacher was saying by this until I started working as a hypnotherapist.

What it means to me is that your mind can only consciously hold so much in it at any given time without you going nuts. There is a lot of information stored there in your brain, but you cannot possibly hold it in your mind at once – it's just too much!

The unconscious mind, as I explain to clients, to me is like a camcorder, or video recorder. Let's say you stop reading this for a moment and begin to pan your eyes around the four walls of the room you're sitting in or the four directions of the park or outdoor space you are in. Moving slowly, or not, since it is not necessary how fast or slow you do it, you're eyes are like the lenses of a camera and you are slowly taking in every single thing around you. The thing is, though, that unless I specifically ask you what main object is directly to your right, you may not hold that in your mind. Once I ask about that, though, it is pulled up so you can recall it – just like a memory.

The other way to think of it is that your mind is like a computer with many files and folders in it. Unless you go into the main section called 'Documents' and ask for the file with your name on it you have to keep selecting things and narrowing things down until you are finally able to open the exact file with the exact information you want. I think, as do many psychologists, that your brain works the same way. You are only able to pull up what you ask for or direct yourself to. In this philosophy, the brain and the mind are the tools through which you view other worlds and time periods.

This gets back to the question asked at the beginning of this section – how are the rules created to tell you who you used to be and why and how did the higher power decided on how many times you came back as opposed to others.

This is a question that has no answer. What this book will attempt to do is take a look at some of the possibilities as to what is really going on here and how the rules may change as our consciousness expands and is capable of considering new ideas.

Some of these things you are about to read will challenge long held beliefs you may hold about the nature of reality.

Like any thing we choose to look at on this earth, I believe we do not necessarily have any answer to any question with any certainty. As we evolve mankind is continually evolving and learning better ways of doing things and new ways of being. The intent of my study is to open doors to new possibilities and new ways of thinking.

The more I live, as I have previously reported, the more I believe we do not really understand our own nature. Just like the quantum computer, the machine, meaning you and me, cannot fully understand itself – ever. And why would we want to? The search makes our lives have meaning.

Life is the journey to explore and attempt to come to higher understanding, but if man created even the scientific method that we hold so dear, then how can we know it is correct? How can we know for sure that the things we now believe are real? Evolution is a process in which we open ourselves up to new ways of being.

As we explore the rules of the intelligent design or source that created all things, I hope we can continue to keep an open mind so that new and better ways of being may be discovered.

Twenty Five
Present

The more I go on in my work, the more I am convinced that to define the psi phenomenon reported on in books as being based solely on past lives is simply not correct.

I realize this is not something all of my clients want to hear me say, but because I have worked with so many people these past several years, and have seen firsthand the depths stored within our subconscious minds, I am not convinced that past lives are real, or I should say, I'm not convinced this definition fits all that is happening here. As with anything, I believe the more we learn about things the more we have more answers and the past several years of research for me have provided many more quesions than answers in regards to this question.

What if all time really is right now and you and I are connected to the same field of energy comprising everything in our known universe and through that, the things we tap into in altered states are more a reflection of some collective thought?

Swiss psychiatrist, Carl Jung, may have been more in tune with reality than just about anyone in the course of history through his theories of archetypes and the collective consciousness, Jung helped define the way we all identify with certain ideas and concepts that seem universal to us all.

When ideas become part of the larger culture, everyone has access to them energetically and in many cases, I think this is what people are tapping into when they are in hypnotic states.

Again, whether they are past lives or just symbolic messages from the subconscious, the reason why I believe in past life therapy is because it helps the person get up out of themselves and their lives and see things from a new perspective so they can easily release old patterns, accept themselves at a greater level and experience more peace through understanding.

To limit ourselves, though, by insisting that past lives are the only way to explain this phenomenon would be doing injustice to us all as we continue our evolution.

Twenty Six
Future Memories

You hopefully recall in the earlier section on time travel how easy it is for you to travel into your future, at least to lunch tomorrow, to see what you will be doing.

The concept of the future is for many of us even more stressful and anxiety ridden than hanging on to the past. One of the main reasons people seek any kind of intuitive advice is because they are unsure about the future and this has certainly been the case in my private practice. These days, most people need a session to clarify their path and experience their highest vision of themselves and all they are capable of creating.

Usually when I work in futures, it is to help people get a clearer picture of their career goals. One woman who owns a retreat center decided to have a session to gain clarity on her next steps in business and found a very exciting and fulfilling future awaited her:

"I am on a stage. There is a podium and spot-lights," she said. "Now I'm looking through the eyes of someone else and she is checking the microphone to prepare for the workshop that's about to begin," she said.

"What year is this?" I asked.

"It's not too far from right now," she said, "maybe five years from now."

"How do you feel?" I asked.

"Confident, proud of what I've been able to do," she said.

"What were the first steps you took to get to this place where you are now?" I asked.

"First, I created these meditation groups over the years and was involved with a group project in Hawaii to start later this year and I am writing content of the website and designing the newsletter."

"Good, and how do you feel now that you've accomplished all of this?" I asked.

"I'm at the point that I can be less attached to the outcome so I feel very peaceful about the

whole thing," she said. "I'm okay with just speaking and writing what I know to be true today and now I am feeling more connected to the person on the stage. "

"Good, now I want you to imagine you can become totally connected with the you who is on the stage, looking out her eyes and feeling what she feels. Let me know when you're there." I said.

"I'm there," she said.

"Good, and how do you feel?"

"Powerful, like there is nothing I can't do."

In this case study, it is interesting to note that for a moment, the woman was actually able to become someone else, one of her assistants who was helping her out.

This suggests it may be easier than we think to actually tap into the thoughts, feelings and actions of someone else, and if that is the case, it makes me wonder even more whether the 'past lives' we visit in hypnosis are actually our own, or if they are just lives of others who have come before us that help us to demonstrate a lesson we are experiencing in the now.

There is no way to know with any certainty how it all works. Maybe we do tap into our own past lives sometimes, but I would imagine in other instances, we are actually living through others in order to understand the self.

There is a web of consciousness that underlies all things in the universe and by tapping into that, we can be available to discover the feelings of anything or anyone in existence throughout time.

Twenty Seven
The Distant Future

In a few instances, clients go beyond this life and travel thousands of years into the future sharing detailed accounts of what is coming to pass through the ages.

I first considered this idea after talking to famed regression therapist, Dr. Brian Weiss, about this. He told me that he had taken people to lives thousands of years from now, although it was something I had never worked with before until I began to occasionally stumble on it by accident. That is the exciting part of this work – you never know what is within someone's mind and what they will come up with.

I believe your mind always presents what you most need to experience, and some-times, for some people, that is a lifetime yet to come.

The most profound of these cases is from a man who came to my workshop on parallel universes and went through the process listed in the first section of the book. Instead of traveling into the distant past, or to a time frame close to our own, he went way out in the future to chronicle eras currently unknown to us.

First he reported on the year 2036:

"We are underwater and preparing to leave our homes to seek new worlds. Some embark on a journey to prepare the new world energetically, while others seek a more solid presence."

Next, he traveled to the year 2900:

"I see a mountainous world new, clear and pure and we are at a very high elevation. We are preparing a system which will allow us to co-exist in harmony with this world from the most non-invasive state possible."

Next, a glimpse into 3400:

"The structures are crystalline and integrated with existing life. We have become the structures themselves, much more so than in other realities."

And finally, a look at 4108:

"It's hard to explain. It's like we are nearing unification with planetary consciousness."

Although it sounds like the stuff of sci-fi, according to this account, our consciousness will continue to expand through the ages until we are back at the source and not separate from it. Interesting things to consider, for sure!

Reality leaves a lot to the imagination.

– John Lennon

PART THREE
CHANGING REALITY

Deep unspeakable suffering may well be called a baptism, a regeneration, the initiation into a new state.

– George Eliot

Twenty Eight
The Root of All Suffering

The more I work with people the more I am convinced that the root of all suffering lies in the way we view reality.

If we dwell on the past, beat ourselves up over past losses and defeats, or refuse to let go and move on, chaos ensues in our minds and ultimately our bodies.

Like many others in this field, I believe our illnesses begin first with a thought, a stress, a tragedy, grief unresolved, and then eventually work their way into our bodies.

I don't know that it is possible to completely avoid illness and suffering in the world. Even those who feel they are 'on the path' to self discovery and healing still find themselves falling pray to the world around us, and that is okay.

We are here to have a physical experience and illness is certainly part of that.

My goal is to figure out how to help people avoid illness altogether, or at least transform certain energies into new patterns of thought and feeling that will support maximum health and vitality.

How we do that is with our thinking, although as I've said again and again in this book, the machine cannot understand itself, and certainly that is the case with you and I.

Haven't you ever noticed that when you are in the middle of crisis you have to ask a friend for advice? I'm sure we've all done it. I think it is because we cannot fully see ourselves the way others can.

It is important during these times that the person we consult is at least as reasonable and wise as we are. I heard a motivational speaker once say you should never take advice from anyone more screwed up than you are, and I think that's true!

You actually have all the answers within you, somewhere, yet when life gets in the way, it's hard to hear that inner voice sometimes, that loving guidance we all have.

That is why I love the field of hypnotherapy because you turn to the hypnotherapist not as a guru or someone with gifts and talents beyond your own, but more of as a facilitator who can objectively assist you into the realm of your own subconscious mind where you can get

answers from yourself which is quite empower-
ing.

    The other thing hypnosis can do is allow
you to take a look at things from a new perspective, with a new pair of glasses, so to speak, so
that you can let go of things that are upsetting
and find greater degrees of peace.

    When you are able to shift reality,
suffering comes to an end.

As far as we can discern, the sole purpose of human existence is to kindle a light in the darkness of mere being.

– Carl Jung

Twenty Nine
Collective Conscious of Carl Jung

After years in the psychotherapy field, Swiss born philosopher Carl Jung developed the philosophy of the collective conscious, which I mentioned briefly in the last chapter.

The longer I am in this field the more I think Jung's work is perhaps some of the most significant in history when it comes to understanding the mind and the way we are all connected to one another.

Through Jung's work on archetypes, we now have a framework to understand why some ideas and concepts are seemingly universal in nature. For example, if I mention a cowboy to you, you will most likely conjure up a vision of a man in a hat and boots riding a horse across the desert, gun holster strapped to his hip.

If I mention pirate to you, these days you will probably think of the actor Johnny Depp, who has practically become a new archetype for your older vision of a man with a peg leg, patch over one eye who rides the seas searching for treasure.

A damsel in distress brings to mind a beautiful young woman, probably with long hair, and finely dressed trapped in a tower made of stone.

Archetypal energies are endless and speak a universal language that break down cultural barriers and speak to each of us at a deep subconscious level.

When I am doing past life regression, I occasionally wonder if what the person is recalling is actually a past life, or merely the energy of one of the myriad archetypes.

One woman seemed to tap into several archetypal energies during a past life regression:

"I am in Boston in the 1700's," she said. "I see an old crone, and my head is being covered and I am being persecuted because of my learning and teaching. I see witches garb like the kind you see on Halloween. I'm not able to trust anyone."

When I asked the woman to move to another place in time, she arrived somewhere and reported the following:

"I am a nun in a habit, again, I am being persecuted," she said.

"Is this a pattern for you, yes or no?" I asked.

"Yes," she said, without hesitation.

"How many lifetimes have you been persecuted – the first number that comes to your mind." I said.

"Thirty-nine," she said, without hesitation.

"Good, now imagine that you can quickly see many or all of these thirty-nine lives and tell me what they are. Imagine they are passing through your mind very quickly."

"I see an old crone with one glowing eye," she said.

"What is the significance of that?" I asked.

"It will be there no matter what form I take," she said.

"Good, so what else do you see?"

"I lived in the times of the Romans, Christ, I see a sheik with the head gear, shepherds," she paused. "There are many costumes, I don't know what they are and don't have words to describe them. A gypsy, mother, a Jewish person, fairies..."

"Good, so what lessons did you learn from that?" I asked.

"The only time it was safe was when it was a woman dominated society," she said.

Hearing stories like the one above with fairies and crones eventually began to pique my curiosity about these things.

Recently, I decided to experiment with a group and take them consciously into a space where they could more consciously identify any archetypes they are working with in their lifetimes. The results were pretty interesting!

One woman discovered her soul purpose:

"I am a guardian, guide, priest, holder of the collective female wisdom of the family. The lesson of that is that I have the responsibility now to guide others and that is my soul purpose, to teach, to guide."

Another man discovered his inner child:

"I was wearing a blue set of pajamas and I was barefooted jumping on a bed. I was very comfortable and I was just jumping on that bed like a little child."

One woman discovered her power:

"I was a she-devil. I wore a tight red outfit and held a pitch fork. As the cosmos opened up, I was transformed into a male warrior with angel wings and the lower body of a horse. I merged him into me and I experienced the power I had been trying to find through sexuality."

Another woman saw herself in a helpful light:

"I was like some kind of leprechaun or elf. I was a helper and my purpose is to help people to see and know things. I'm talking about Universal knowing and integration into self-knowing. Not through the brain and that's okay, it's just how I am wired. More direct and flowing through me, a more direct link."

One woman was a queen:

"I am in a Queen's dress. I'm a semi heavy queen with white skin and I am wearing a golden very fancy dress with heavy fabric lined with royal blue and wearing golden pointy shoes with a narrow tip rolled up like a snail. It's very fancy and relates to my present live about loving myself."

Whether these people actually were who they reported to be or whether they were merely tapping into an archetypal realm is not for us to judge. The bottom line in this form of work is to dig into our deepest subconscious aspects to reshape our view of reality.

When that is done and people find more meaning and happiness in their lives in the here and now, that is when the work is successful.

Thirty
Accessing Anything
We Want Right Now

In theory, I have long believed we have
the ability to access any time, place or person
we want to simply by 'traveling' in our minds to
do so, as mentioned briefly in the earlier section
on future memories.

What do I mean by that? I believe we
can visit ancient times, meet with brilliant
minds or gain access to sacred knowledge by
somehow accessing that in our minds, via
hypnosis, meditation or the dream state.

Recently, I had the opportunity to experiment with this idea. A man came to see me who
was working as a professional cyclist. His mind
was very sharp and I could tell he truly had the
demeanor of a champion.

Although he was quite successful already and was cycling as part of a nationally
sponsored team, he wanted to use some of the

future memory techniques discussed earlier in the book as a means to get his ultimate goals accomplished – a world championship.

As the session began and he was talking, I got the idea that it would be powerful for him to be able to tap into some of the world's great champions before him at the very first Olympic Games in Athens, Greece.

He traveled back in time and I asked him to float down into the event:

"Look around and tell me what you see, or what's happening," I said.

"People are in the coliseum," he said, "waiting for the next event."

"And what is that?" I asked.

"I see stone holes," he said.   "Oh, it's the javelin."

'What are you doing there?   Are you participating in any way?"

"No, I'm just watching it from the bleachers," he said.

"How does it feel there?" I asked.

"I can feel the excitement and the anticipation of the crowd and all the energy there," he said.

"How many people are there?"

"Oh, thousands and thousands," he said.

"Imagine you can fast forward through the day and arrive at the next event and tell me what it is."

"It's the one where they throw the rock. I forget what it's called. Oh yeah, it's the discus," he said.

"Tell me about the awards ceremony. Are they all recognized at once?"

"No," he said, "they stand up after each event and have crowns put on their heads."

"Fast forward now to the next event and tell me about that."

"They're running a race around the coliseum. It looks like this is what the people have been waiting for," he said.

"What is it like to watch?"

"As they're running they are so happy as they finish and the people are loud and cheering."

"What happens after that?"

"That is the last event," he said, "the people finish for the day after the awards are given out."

"I want you to imagine the champions of each of the competitions – the javelin, discus and race. Imagine you can see them all lined up and notice which of them looks or feels the most passionate, disciplined and successful to you and let me know which one that is," I said.

"The runner," he said.

"Good. Now imagine you can walk or float over to the runner. What is he like? How does he feel right now?"

"He feels amazed that he accomplished what he set out to do," he said.

"Good. Now imagine you can float over to him and float right down into him and see what he feels like now."

"Amazed," he said.

"Good. Now I want to know what makes him different from all the others. Why did he win and they did not?"

"He has an inner strength. He is determined. He had to win," he said.

"Why was that? For financial reasons, or spiritual reasons or both?"

"It was just within him. It was something he had to do more for spiritual reasons," he said.

"Good. Now I want you to imagine you can feel his strength and resolve and allow it to fill up your entire being starting with the tips of your toes and going all the way up to the top of your head. You are becoming strong and full of resolve and inner strength."

The client made an energetic shift as I guided him through this process and through the rest of the session. Interestingly, this session shows something I have always thought about – that we can be or do anything we want to do simply by tapping into the storehouse of information and energy currently available to us on any realm of existence we choose.

If you want to meet JFK, for example, I believe you could go there. If you're dream was to become an astronaut, I believe you could do that too, simply using your mind.

One client came to the office who was an avid fan of Marilyn Monroe and wanted to meet her.

After guiding her through relaxation, she went into a beautiful room where a door opened and Marilyn walked through the door and said hello.

"Imagine she could walk up to you and tell you anything you need to know at this time. What will you ask her?"

"I want to know why I have been having these dreams about her for the past several years," she said.
"And what is her answer?" I asked.

"She says it's because she wants me to help her tell the world what really happened to her," she said.

"Imagine she can tell you now," I said.

The client sat quietly for a moment and finally spoke. "She's telling me that I will know it in time when she is ready to tell it, but that it is nothing like any of the theories currently out there in the public or media," she said.

"When will it be time to know this?" I asked.

"In a few years," she said.

"Does it have anything to do with JFK," I asked.

"No," she said.

"Will she tell you anything else about it now?"

"No," she said.   "She will let me know when."

"How will she do that?" I asked.

"Dreams," she said.   "She will visit me in my dreams."

"And it will be easy for you to recall these dreams," I said.

"Yes, it will," she agreed.

I hope to hear the end of that story, for sure! Again, we can only speculate on exactly what the woman is tapping into – is it reality or is it merely a fantasy in her own mind, or both?

The point is that it really doesn't matter as long as it brings greater clarity to life.

Creativity is a drug I cannot live without.
     – Cecil B. DeMille (1881–1959)

Thirty One
The Realm of Creativity

I am interested in creativity and where it comes from. Particularly in the literary world, there have been so many amazing works of creative fiction – everything from the *Harry Potter* Books, to *Star Wars* to the books by Tolkien and the *Lord of the Rings*, creative efforts runneth over in the world of Hollywood.

When you see Sci-Fi in general, don't you ever stop to wonder where these creative minds came up with all of this stuff? How could somebody possibly imagine some of the strange creatures and far away lands portrayed in today's fiction genre?

A couple of years ago, I decided to go to Dragon Con, the world's largest Science Fiction convention in Atlanta. I thought it may be a good way to promote my book *Beyond Reality*.

Little did I know that reality was the last thing the attendees were thinking about.

When I arrived, I could not believe my eyes! Sure, I had seen Sci-Fi and Trekkie gatherings on TV before, but nothing could quite prepare me for what I encountered there. So many people dressed in costume and in character, living out their wildest fantasies as Storm Troopers, Intergalactic Beings and Fairy Princesses. It was quite a site to behold!

During the four day conference there were several sessions where you could meet with Sci-Fi TV celebrities and hear amazing stories about how these shows and books are created.

I decided to spend most of my time attending writer's workshops and I happened to have the opportunity to hear Ann Crispin who wrote many of the New York Times bestselling *Star Trek* books.

As would be expected in any gathering like this, during Q & A time, an audience member asked her the most common question, "So how do you come up with your ideas?"

The common question had a common answer yet the way she said it took me by surprise. "I *channeled* it," she said. "It just comes to me. I don't really know how."

Channeling is such a New Age term I nearly fell out of my chair, and to have someone with such high credibility use that term was quite astounding to me.

When I looked the term up in the dictionary, there were several revealing definitions to ponder:

1. A course or pathway through which information is transmitted: new channels of thought; a reliable channel of information.

2. In communications theory, a gesture, action, sound, written or spoken word, or   visual image used in transmitting information

3. A temporary opening in a cell membrane that allows ions or molecules to pass into or out of the cell.

4. The medium through which a spirit guide purportedly communicates with the physical world.

It is interesting to think of this term in all its more scientific applications, particularly the third entry which supposes that the channel allows ions to pass through it. As I have said before, I think our thoughts are real things, occupying real space and if that is true, then perhaps we actually do bring ions or molecules through us as information or ideas are allowed to flow into physical reality.

Years ago, I tried my hand at fiction writing. It was actually by accident that it happened. I was vacationing on a cruise ship at the time, sitting on the deck working on my tan when I began to see a little movie running in my head.

It was a heavy set older man who was sitting at the slot machine in a smoky bar on board a ship. I did not know what it meant, so I ignored it for a day, but the next day, I saw it again, only the details were a bit clearer and the scene ran longer than before.

I began to think this may be of some importance, so I took out my journal, which I rarely travel without, and began to write down exactly what I saw there, the look of the room and what the man was doing and saying. Before long, I was 'channeling' a story about a murder on a cruise ship which later turned into a 100,000 word manuscript complete with several sets of twisted characters and plots.

Where this came from, I had no idea. A clearer answer, or at least some form of validation, occurred when I picked up a copy of a great book called *On Writing* by Stephen King. This is his memoirs and in it, he described in great detail some of the things I had been experiencing in my own life.

King mentioned the fact that anytime he attempted to plot his books, he felt they were never as good as if he just let the characters tell him what they would do and not the other way around.

If that is the case, then who are these people, where are they from and why are they handing down all this information? Could it be that they are real people who exist on another dimension of reality who find a lending ear to which they can tell their tales of triumph and woe? We can only speculate.

If you think of this idea, though, you realize that many famous people, songwriters, artists, architects or others, when asked, all seem to say they have no idea where their 'inspiration comes from. They just saw their creation in their mind's eye, already finished and immediately began work on it.

Particularly in the world of hypno-therapy, so much of what the client is able to experience is dependent upon their willingness to engage in the creative process of allowing their visions to come through and to express those verbally. Clients are continually surprised to discover that the things they created for themselves during a session can ultimately have a profound impact on the quality of their life, maybe that same day, but maybe some weeks or months later. If they allow themselves to be open to possibility and the creative part of the mind, that aspect of the self will allow them to unfold their highest potential and destiny in the conscious plane.

Leprechauns, castles, good luck and laughter. Lullabies, dreams and love ever after. Poems and songs with pipes and drums. A thousand welcomes when anyone comes... That's the Irish for you!

Thirty Two
Unicorns & Leprechauns –
Fact or Fiction?

Earlier, you saw a case history of someone who experienced her archetypal self as an elf or Leprechaun. Because I hear things like this quite often, and the more I think about the source of all the supposed 'imaginary' beings we create in our minds, the more I am convinced these things must exist somewhere out there in space and time, perhaps on another dimension of reality altogether.

I've worked with several clients who have gone into vivid details of these other worlds, including the woman who recalled how she receives spontaneous past life recall. She went into vivid details about her life in the faerie realm:

*"When I was 33 a psychic told me very offhand-
edly that I was heavily involved with the faeries
in another life. While I didn't actually remember what I was envisioning as she spoke, it
didn't seem impossible to me. I started to
ponder it, and what was coming into my mind
wasn't little gossamer winged beings, however I
was getting clear visions of a time and place
that was much too real to ignore.*

*Then, I had a near stranger literally blurt out on
our second meeting that he thought I came from
a place and a time where beings lived that were
not human and not angels called in earthly
terms the Tuatha De Danaan in Ireland. The
little fairy people reside in the dimension where
these beings now reside, outside of the earthly
realm. The coincidence of what he was saying
was also compelling, so I didn't automatically
reject the idea while I may have if I hadn't
already had some exposure to the notion.*

*Rapidly, I began having visions in my dreams of
people, places, and times that included the
things the previous people had mentioned and
other things that my mind would not ordinarily
come up with in a daydream, or even if I was to
write a fictional story. I am quite aware there is
a thin line between enlightenment and delusion,
so I tried to be careful to not let my mind drift
and wander when I had these visions. Shortly
after, some people from this past life were*

visiting with me in dreams, although what they were saying seemed to not be as important as the fact they were "with" me. I knew I was on the right track.

The most significant memories to me were about where I came from BEFORE the fairy life. It had to do with the "fall in heaven" as described in the bible, where there was a parting of ways and ideas. I don't actually recall being there, but being affected by the fallout. I believe that I am descended some of the original beings that fell and do not incarnate. I know what it's like to love them even though they now have dank, dark energies. I also have a connection to entities, related to those beings, who did not fall and have bright light energies that would blind you if you looked at them. The two are closely related, one group just went one way and one another long, long time ago. This was not planned in the creation of the universe, and was a huge hiccup in things. Because of this division I usually did not live with people who were my "family", whatever that means. I came into the earth dimension with the 2nd wave or group of beings who came this way at the time of the creation of the planet. I suspect that some in the 1st group were ones who fell, but I'm not positive. The 1st group were planners, the 2nd group was the crew who actually did things."

Another client reported extremely vivid

accounts of her life as a variety of otherworldly
beings while being guided through the parallel
universe journey you saw earlier in the book:

*"I went up the elevator and as the levels
changed, I started to become the angel that was
with me. As I got off the elevator, the higher
power greeted me and passed energy over my
chest illuminating it completely, the energy
passed over me again and it returned, and it
went away. It was like a game to show me that
there was no difference between us. I was the
angel, the angel was me. I was still complete
and perfect.*

*I asked this being if I was in a parallel universe
and was told I was not, but I was able to project
myself to different astral planes, coming and
going as I liked.*

*The first path looked like Edward Hughes
'Midsummer's Eve' painting. It was a land of
fairies, all feminine energy, and we laughed and
played and had fun.*

*On the second path I became a mermaid with
long red hair. I had a male counterpart and we
played and swam around.*

*On the third path, I was a belly dancer and this
same man in the mermaid vision was romanti-
cally connected to me.*

The final path was he and I again as Native Americans at the end of our lives, happily curled up together watching the show fall from the warmth of our teepee and fire."

Who's to say that the places these people visited are any more or less real than where we are today on planet earth. I believe these folks are tapping into worlds in other times, spaces and universes. Perhaps the wisdom we receive in such spaces can assist us right now.

As we move forward in time, the illusion that it is, I believe understanding the creative realm is key to not only creating the world we really want to live in, but to actually save and expand humanity as we know it.

Oh my God! Space aliens! Don't eat me, I have a wife and kids! Eat them.

— Homer Simpson
Treehouse of Horror VII

Thirty Three
Aliens from Outer Space

People often ask me if I have regressed those who believe they have been abducted by aliens and the answer to that is 'yes,' but I normally tend to discover people who claim they themselves were once from other planets.

One of the most interesting involved a woman who came to me to get clarification on the source of her weight issues, which she had struggled with all her life:

"Where are you?" I asked.

"Not on Earth," she said, "It feels like the entire landscape was barren and all the creatures were starving in this place. Some major disaster happened, a natural disaster. Everything is dead as far as foliage and things that

grow. I'm starving to death and angry because this was preventable."

"Are you also scared?"

"No," she said. "The anger is pretty much pushing out the fear."

"How is this affecting you now?" I asked.

"This is the source of where my weight problem began. I felt like I would starve and it's like I am trying to fill this space up so I won't go hungry again," she said. "But it also has some positive effects on what I do now. I enjoy shaking things up and calling a spade a spade and telling people how I see things. I am a letter writer and I do send angry emails when I think people need to hear my views. I am frustrated in this life just like I was back then because I feel so many people are asleep and they are not aware of how they're participating in the ruination of planet Earth."

"Imagine you can rewind to the events prior to your starvation and see the path that led the civilization to that place of destruction," I said.

"I was a scientist in a lab or something like that," she said. "I anticipated what was coming and tried to warn everyone, only they would not listen. It was some kind of meteor that had

impacted our planet, but we had the technology to stop it, but nobody listened."

"How did this make you feel?" I asked.

"I was the laughing stock among my peers they thought I did not know what I was talking about. I tried to take it to the people and they didn't believe me. I felt like there was something I could've done to get the point across. I felt pain and humiliated by the way I was treated by my peers," she said.

Another woman came for a session who said for years she had a vision of a green colored being in her mind that scared her:

"Sometimes when I close my eyes to meditate, I would see this thing," she said. "It is so scary, I decided to stop meditating altogether and now I feel like I am missing out on something if I don't start trying to meditate again."

After putting her in a safe space via hypnosis, I had her imagine the green being came up to her to have a talk:

"He is my guide," she said, "He's trying to help me with things; only I haven't wanted to listen because of the way he looks. I will allow him to help me now. There is nothing to be scared of."

"Where is he from?" I asked.

"From no place around here," she said.   "I really don't know."

"What kind of things is he helping you with?" I asked.

"He says he will tell me in time, but not right now. I have to start to meditate again and things will be shown to me," she said.

People wonder if I believe in life on other planets and I absolutely do. How could we be so egotistical to think that in a universe as vast as ours that we are the only living things God created? That makes no sense.

I believe that the people who glimpse into these other worlds are able to tap into a new perspective and higher wisdom that can aid us here with our own issues and challenges on earth and that is a good thing.

We could say these people are merely expressing a highly imaginative, creative side of themselves, but again, I say it does not matter if it conforms to our current definitions of reality or not. What matters is how the information is used to enhance life.

Thirty Four
Mentally Ill or Superbly Psychic?

Speaking of those more creative than the average, I am continually fascinated by psychological disorders, particularly schizophrenia.

Did you see the film *The Beautiful Mind* with Russell Crowe? This movie documented the life of mathematical genius, John Nash and his inner quest to dispel the horrors of schizophrenia. In the film, we see how the man has a couple of people who follow him around and talk to him, although they are invisible to everyone else.

At one critical moment in the film, Nash suddenly notices that these people are always talking about the same things and while he notices himself aging in the mirror along with his wife and everyone else around him, he wonders why his companions stay the same age, always wear the same clothes and seem to come out of nowhere talking about the same things all the time.

In that moment, he wakes from the dream, so to speak and realizes that in order for these people to go away, he only need to ignore them and eventually they stop talking to him almost entirely so he is able to maintain a relatively normal life free of his anti-psychotic medications.

Reading about potential causes of this ailment which affects millions of Americans, there was a theory that the schizophrenic person has more dopamine in their brain than a normal person. In fact, we could say the brain is practically flooded with it.

An experiment I would love to conduct, although I have no idea how I ever would get permission for such a thing, would be to take perfectly 'normal' people and somehow flood their brains with dopamine to see if this would cause them to hallucinate also, or as I prefer to see it, allow the veil between the worlds to thin a bit.

It is my theory that what we would create by doing this would be a bunch of super psychics who would be able to see all of the beings and entities that are probably surrounding each one of us right now.

If it is true that our planet is experiencing actual vibrational frequency shifts, then it would seem probable that as we undergo such earth changes, that our perceptions of reality would also change. I believe that all things are right around us yet so many of them are currently unperceivable to our minds and our current abilities.

Those self proclaimed psychics who can supposedly see the dead and carry on lengthy conversations with them are no different than you or me; it's just that somehow they have an innate ability to perceive the unperceivable and do things that you and I can also do with practice. If these people are also 'hearing voices' shouldn't they also be institutionalized and labeled with a diagnosis of schizophrenia according to the rules of society? I think not! I have had the opportunity to work with several clients who have been officially diagnosed with 'schizo-affective disorder,' yet when I talk to them they seem perfectly normal to me, usually just far more brilliant than the average person. There is probably a thin line between delusion and normal reality and for some, it may take more of an effort to be normal. I have received some incredibly bizarre letters these past few years, and this one I received after I was on Coast to Coast AM is worth sharing as we discuss the subject of sanity. I will include our correspondence here:

"Hello,

I am a refugee/agent from an alternate reality/universe/dimension (RUD). In my RUD my earth was ravaged by bio-terrorist. Almost all life was destroyed and I was saved by an being who offered me a deal. In exchange for a new life in this RUD, I would help make changes; sometimes very small, sometimes large to other RUDs. I have been married to royalty and stopped terrorism on a planetary scale. I have bought a stamp and mailed a letter and moved on to the next RUD. I am finally through with my service and live in this RUD. My memory was supposed to have been wiped but it only partially worked. I am happy here because this RUD is what mine should have been if not for Bin Laden. You are correct that there are an infinite amount of RUDs. There are RUDs where 1 electron on the other side of the RUD spins a tiny bit different than this one and that is the ONLY difference. There are ones where you had one cup of coffee this morning instead of 2 and that is all. There are RUDs where our galaxy doesn't exist. There are RUDs that are composed of only blackness and void. There are infinite combinations of every other kind of RUD. I gave you my email if you want to respond, but Smith is not my real name. I have to keep away from my hometown because there is another one of me there. It's kind of like the witness protection program."

I sent a brief reply:

"So there is another you in your hometown? Interesting!"

Here was the response:

"Yes. He lives totally unaware of my existence. This RUD's version of all my friends, family & relatives are alive and well. As part of the terms of my relocation to this RUD, contact of any kind is not allowed. I just hope no type of biometric ID will become standard in this RUD or it may raise some flags..."

"You mean like an implanted monitoring device??" I replied.

He responded:

"No. Biometrics ID devices are, for example, unique identifiers like fingerprints, retinas, or even a person's bioelectric signature. If my "doppelganger" in this RUD ever registers his, for example, fingerprints, then since I have the exact same prints as he does, I would have to be very careful about when or even if I ever register or use mine. It would be the ULTIMATE form of identity theft."

Sometime much later he wrote again with the following:

"I read my hometown newspaper on line the other day and saw my doppelganger (he is native to this reality) got a speeding ticket. I read where he got it at and remember speeding

through that area when I was younger. Gives me tingles."

Super psychic or super psychotic – you be the judge!

I recall my first Reiki teacher telling me that she was institutionalized for some time after telling her family that she could speak to the dead.

I'm sure many in my field were closer to getting hauled off in the paddy wagon than they would care to remember.

I think the society fears that which it cannot understand and just because someone displays exceptional gifts and unique talents, something will have to be done to learn to work with these folks rather than locking them up.

Worlds of information are available to us through these special people if we can only open up and allow them to teach us what they know.

It's as if they have special filters through which they view things and I believe they have much to contribute to society at large.

Thirty Five
Visions of the Blind

Recently I was asked if I'd ever worked with the blind, which I have had the opportunity to do.

My client had been legally blind since birth and to date can only perceive shadows and shapes.

For this writing, I wanted to talk to him in further detail about his experience of hypnosis and get more details about how he was able to visualize things during this process:

"It happens in two ways," he said, "Either it is something I have seen before with my limited sight, or some things I see in full color but they are nothing I have ever actually seen before. It's like I use my mind's eye to visualize things. I guess I see what I want to see, I see with my heart. I can listen to the sound of someone's voice to figure out how they feel and that brings

an image to my mind."

"Are the images in color?" I asked.

"Yes, almost always," he said.

"Where do you think these things come from?"

"To me they are like a river that flows down from some place outside of myself and fork off into different streams of possibility. It's hard to explain, really."

We've seen evidence of this higher level of being with superstars such as Stevie Wonder or Ray Charles, or the amazing Helen Keller.

The fact that one of the senses is not available does not seem to be a detriment to experiencing things visually.

To me, it suggests that there may be a deeper knowing of the soul, a memory one can tap into at any given moment and know about the all that is.

Where these memories may come from is the subject of the next section of the book.

PART FOUR
GENETIC MEMORY

Thinking: The talking of the soul
with itself.

                          – Plato

Thirty Six
"Great Minds Think Alike"

Through the years, I've come to believe that the things that go on in our minds can be explained by something other than past lives.

I think it has to do with a sort of genetic memory we share with all of mankind for all time.

What if you and I are picking up information and feelings from times gone by or times yet to come?

There is much being written at this time about this very real possibility.

You and I may be more linked to our ancestors and to mankind as a whole than we had ever previously imagined.

This next section will explore some of the evidence I've uncovered to support this theory.

In every work of genius we recognize our own rejected thoughts: they come back to us with a certain alienated majesty.

– Ralph Waldo Emerson

Thirty Seven
Anatomy of a Thought

Have you ever stopped to wonder how you are able to think? How does a thought come to you? I would imagine as you read this your mind is searching for the answer, perhaps the way your computer searches for a lost file. It's in there somewhere, right?

When I teach psychic development classes, I often ask my students to stop and think about where their thoughts come from. The point of psychic development is to try to develop senses other than the main five of sight, sound, taste, touch and smell.

When a thought enters your mind it takes effort to stop and think about where it came from. For example if I ask you to remember the first place you ever lived, you may recall a picture of it in your mind, or the feeling of how you felt there.

That information is already in your mind so you can simply recall it and be back in that moment.

But what if you are trying to tap into other realms or dimensions of reality? The first thing I always ask is whether or not the thought I am having is coming from things I have known before, or does it seem to be from some place outside myself, or outside of what I know up to this point in my life.

Depending on what you ask, you may notice from time to time that you are able to answer questions or just 'know' things that you couldn't have possibly known before, yet somehow the information is there. It is coming in from an extra sensory perception, or ESP.

Where the information is coming from is a question that I don't think we can actually answer. Some intuitives say they are receiving this information from people who are deceased, some say it is from guides, but what if there is another answer – the information is coming from a storehouse of consciousness compiled by the greatest thinkers of all time, and what if you could tap into this wealth of information at any time to get answers to even the most baffling questions. Life could get infinitely easier, I would think.

Most of us have been led to believe the brain stores memories, but recent discoveries suggest that may not be the case.

Thirty Eight
The Man with No Brain

I read an article recently taking about a man who passed away suddenly at a rather young age for no apparent reason. An autopsy was performed and what the coroner found was rather shocking.

The man who had an above average IQ had a brain the size of a fig. Researchers were baffled, to say the least. How could this man function at such a high level without a brain?

This would completely go against everything I have just mentioned about how your brain stores memories. If the brain supposedly stores all that we have ever seen past present and future, how is this possible?

In the last section, my blind client mentioned he could 'see with his heart.' This is not a new concept at all.

There has been much research coming out of the Heart Math Institute in recent years that suggest your heart also has an intelligent system that functions similarly to your brain and that memories are stored there as well as in other parts of the body.

This theory has been the foundation of much of my belief system regarding the use of energy healing. I believe, as many others support, that our memories are stored as holograms in our energetic fields and in our bodies.

If you have every gone to see a massage therapist you know what I am talking about. Have you ever had someone (therapist or not) touch you in a particular place and suddenly you recall something that happened to you a long time ago? I've found this to be the case and to me, it suggests that we really do hold memories in our bodies, which I think is the cause of some illnesses. By holding on to things past, they create an energetic space and that in turn sometimes manifests itself into illness.

There are also hundreds of stories about people who receive transplanted organs and suddenly develop the food cravings or behaviors of the donor.

All of these things lend credibility to the fact that our mind is not limited to the space between our ears.

Thirty Nine
Special Kids or Evolution at Work?

You have probably heard about the Indigo Children, the 'special kids' being born right now. These kids are the ones you keep reading about in the newspapers as being diagnosed as Attention Deficit Hyperactivity Disorder. They are highly intelligent people who are being drugged to keep them under control.

If we believe there is a higher power that created all things, and if you think like I do, that within that higher power came a divine intelligence that guides the living creatures of earth through a process of evolution, would it then not make sense to assume that the people who are being born today are actually more intelligent than we are? If we are truly evolving and getting better, that would make perfect sense.

Of course, the wonders of modern medicine are keeping people alive far longer than natural selection would have allowed, yet more and more these brilliant minds in science and other fields are learning more about the way things work and are passing these brilliant genes on to their offspring.

It makes sense genetically that mankind is continuously evolving to a higher level of being and that perhaps these 'special kids' are able to perceive things that are beyond the capabilities of older people. Perhaps their sixth sense is more developed and they are able to see through the veil in a way that you and I cannot.

That said, if the kids are smarter than we are, is that their fault? No! It is our responsibility as a society to rework our school curriculums to meet the needs of these advanced kids to ensure they are challenged and not getting bored by being forced to learn things the old way. An overhaul of public education is needed, but the answer to these problems does not lie in the hands of a pharmaceutical company!

As we continue to evolve here on earth, we desperately need to expand our current awareness as a society to include the possibility that we really are getting better and brighter and begin to act like it!

Forty
The Sins of the Father

There is an old saying that the sins of the father are replayed on the son. In more modern terms, I recently heard the result of a current study on genetics that says that one-third of how we feel is genetic, meaning it is passed down to us from our parents and ultimately from our ancestors.

If that is the case, then perhaps these bright children have a lot on their plates and some of the more violent outbursts we hear about in everything from temper tantrums to school shootings can be explained by the incredible psychological tension being felt throughout the world at this time. If this study is true, our younger generations are carrying all of our collective feelings with them, and perhaps it is more than they can deal with.

Isn't that amazing to think of? For years I have been teaching people how they are affected by others around them more than they are consciously aware of, my main focus of this being the people we run across on a daily basis, but now, this research suggests that one- third of that is already engrained in us at birth!

In a study at the University of Chicago, evidence suggests that loneliness in particular is something hard wired into the genes and that the usual conclusions that people were anti-social or just shy are not the only reasons a person may feel lonely in a crowd.

The assumption that we are really living out a part of our ancestral heritage is a concept described widely in various indigenous cultures where ancestors are consulted and worshiped and in hypnosis, it is a powerful place to look for healing the self.

There are times in regression therapy that understanding our energetic links to past ancestors can be used as a tool to help people unlock the root cause of illness or the source of emotional pain.

The process is simple: take the person back in time through the history of their ancestors to the source event where a particular hardship or condition was first evident and clear it out at that level. Many times, when the person sees the source of their pain lies in an old injury of a great great grandfather or mother, the situation is immediately alleviated. It is incredible work!

I first discovered this myself by accident.

I was visiting with a close friend one day and could see she was upset about something, but she could not say what it was.

That evening during my meditation, she popped into my mind and as a sort of prayer for peace; I asked what I could do to help. Suddenly my mind flashed into a living room in an era that seemed very long ago. I saw a little girl being scolded by her mother, who had her hair up and was wearing those old cat's eye glasses.

I could feel the pain of the little girl and suddenly recognized her as my friend. I imagined a white light coming into the room, dispelling her mother's anger and bringing peace to the girl.

The next day when I saw my friend again, she said she felt much better and I could see she really did appear to be over whatever was bothering her. That's when I knew the power of making these changes to events long ago and how that could change the energy for all time.

If all time is now, then it makes total sense that to heal something in the deep 'past' would have to affect the now as well as the future.

Over the years when people come for a session, there are times when this type of work is exactly what they need. The following are a few examples of just how transformational this can be.

One man received profound insight and

healing concerning his father. When asked to travel through his ancestral history on his father's side, he became emotional:

"It's devastating," he said, with tears welling in his eyes. "It feels like disaster. Choices have to be made where some will be chosen, and some will be left behind. It's horrible."

"Where are you?"

"I don't know."

"What year is it?"

"I don't know."

"Who is being chosen and how is it done?" I asked.

"They will take the ones they think can survive and leave the weak and young behind. They have many children and they just can't take them all."

"Why are they leaving? What kind of disaster is this?" I asked.

"I want to say it's the 1700's in some village setting. The disaster could be fire, flood, attack, I don't know, I just know it was devastating having to escape."

"Where are they going to?"

"Another land, I don't know where. All I see now is the remainder of those who left."

"Imagine you can fast forward in time to the moment where they arrive at the new destination and see what happens there in this other land," I said.

"The parents are happy to be safe, but the children are angry because the parents didn't take all their brothers and sisters and the younger ones didn't understand. The parents realized it had to be done for their survival and now it's up to the older ones to help with that and to start over and prepare because they know its not over and there's going to be future hard choices to be made and if they're going to continue to live, there's going to be hard choices to make without emotion."

"Fast forward again and see what those choices are," I said.

"It's a very hard life," he said. *"It's on a farm, and as on all farms, animals are raised to be killed to sustain life. There is a war, there is fire and I don't see anything else."*

"As you turn your attention back to those initial events in the 1700's, what is this causing now in

your family tree?" I asked.

"The family has always been very controlling and very controlled with feelings and shut down. They don't let their feelings influence the decision making process. They do things out of necessity. There's no love, there's just labor."

Now the important part of the work is to assist the client in making a shift and releasing some of this heavy energy.

"Imagine a white light pours out over those events in the 1700's and slowly lifts any fear, anger, sadness and grief and let me know when it feels better," I said.

After a minute he finally said, "Okay, it's better now."

"Now imagine you can bring that energy forward in time, healing and releasing this emotion and bringing a new level of peace through all time, accepting and feeling that all is well and let me know when that is better."

"It's better!" he said, finally.

Another woman discovered the source of a shameful family secret:

"This was in the time of the American Indians,"

she said. "It feels like an Indian encampment and the year is 1849. A female was taken to the encampment and she had children with an Indian man, but then she came back to a white settlement and people there were very cruel to her and she was ashamed. She lived with the Indians for a long time before she ever got here, but her shame affected the three children."

"How is this affecting your life now?" I asked.

"Nobody will talk about who this ancestor was. It was a shameful secret that simmers through the family and feels very repressed."

The same client was asked to travel through her mother's ancestry, but instead found herself visiting one of her mother's past lives:

"I see a battle field in Scotland in the 1800's," she said. "This is my mother in another life. She was a man then and was in charge of a very fierce, not even human looking people. There was a lot of devastation and death here and she was unable to save her family and wants to be forgiven."

"Can you tell her she's forgiven?" I asked.

"Yes."

"And will she accept that?"

"Yes," she said.

"Good, so go ahead and have her imagine a white light encompassing the battlefield and washing away the stress and pain from those events and let me know when it feels better," I said.

A few moments later she spoke again, "Okay, she is better now."

"Good," I said. "So how are these past events affecting you now?"

"Through the years it contributed to her feeling of poor self esteem and her feeling inferior intellectually."

One woman met her father who guided her through a critical time in her ancestry:

"I saw my father on the right side of my body and we went and floated together all the way back to the 1750's in Britain where there is a battle and people were wearing bullet belts over their torso. The dead are piled up lying on the floor and this place is affecting our entire family."

I had her imagine a white light healing the events and things became clearer and began to shift for the better:

"The healing energy was given and when we came back to the present I realized the events back then relate to current family events in that during this battle there is a lot of violence, death, miscommunication, lack of understanding and walls are built up around us. People are dead just like in the present. There is a disconnection that exists today. The healing energy was sent to all of my family members now. It feels better."

Another woman saw her mother who helped her understand a fear that actually originated from her family lineage:

"My mother is here and she is taking me back to King David's court. She was a seer and foretold him things he didn't use so she was banished from court."

"How is that affecting your life now?" I asked.

"It is causing an ingrained feeling of fear of 'knowing' things and fear of using psychic powers and of seeing, fear of having a voice and this is something I am dealing with in my life now," she said.

Another woman recalled how she also met her mother who took her back to an ancient battleground:

"My mom was there and took me back to a time of war. It is very frightening and dark. When the light began to shine on the group of people, they were happier by the time we left. It felt much better."

Another woman recalled how she felt more connected after her mother guided her back to a time in 4000 B.C.:

"We became connected, no longer invisible; there was a calm knowingness and a strong connection between us that was not there before."

This type of session can also help people with chronic or genetically inherited illnesses. One woman came to see me because she was fearful of getting an inherited disease:

"I'm scared because I am 43 years old and my mother and grandmother all died before they were fifty of cancer," she said.

The goal was to have her travel back in time to the source event where this illness began to affect the lineage. The woman went back to the late 1500's:

"I see a war, a battle in a field, and lots of

blood. There is a man slumped over in a heap. He's dying a horrible death. He was our ancestor and that energy pattern was passed down to our family"

Another man wanted to heal a history of abuse with his father:

"Go back to a significant event in your father's childhood" I told him, "and tell me what you see there."

"I see my dad in a room sitting on the floor," he said.

"How old is he there?" I asked.

"Oh, about five," he said.

"So what's happening?" I asked.

"He's just sitting there playing with a wooden car and his father is coming in the room, yelling and throwing things around. He's drunk."

"How does the little boy feel?" I asked.

"He's scared. He's crying now. He doesn't know what to do."

"Imagine a white light coming down and surrounding this little boy, and imagine the light

will melt away all the fear and then let me know when it is all gone and feels better," I said.

A few minutes later he said, "Okay, it's better now."

"Good, now imagine you can travel back even further in time to a significant event when your grandfather was a little boy and tell me when you're there and what's going on there."

"I see my grandfather in a room with some other children – his brothers and sisters, I guess," he said. "His mother is coming in and screaming at him. She's spanking his brother and yelling and scaring him. She has a terrible temper."

Again, I had the man bring the white light in to heal the event and this went back for two more generations before we came to the source of the trouble.

"This is a very early time," he said.

"Where is it in the world?" I asked.

"I don't know. It looks like the time of cavemen. Really early," he said.

"So what is happening there?"

"I see a man running from some giant creature. He is scared. He is running for his cave," he said.

"Who's in the cave with him?"

"He is all alone now," he said. "His family is dead. His heart is shut down. He has no feelings anymore."

At this source event, now the real healing can begin as the man brought light and an open heart to this ancient ancestor and carried that light all the way through time to his great grandfather, his grandfather and his father.

"Can you see now why your father acted like he did?" I asked. "Can you see that he was doing the best he could?"

"Yes," he said.

"Can you forgive him now?" I asked.

"Of course," he said.

"Good, then imagine a light traveling through him and feel it as it goes through you, lightening and brightening every cell, every part of your being," I said.

Another client wanted to get to the root

of a deep fear she had her whole life and went back in time to her great, great, great grandfather being beat up in an alley and robbed:

"He's getting out of his buggy," she said, "walking toward the building and a man jumped out and hit him in the stomach. It hurts," she said, grabbing her own stomach.

"Then what happened?"

"Now I see him and he's in bed, recovering; only he never really recovers from it. His stomach is always in a knot from then on, he is scared and he dies of some kind of complication from an ulcer," she said.

After imagining a healing light transcending all generations the woman said her fear had melted away. "To this day, it has never returned," she wrote, in a subsequent email.

Are we really that connected to those who have come before us? I would imagine that we are. We may actually be forever connected to each other through some kind of genetic memory.

Forty One
Theory on How Genetic
Memory Works

Looking back at the last section on creativity and how we have the ability, in my opinion, to access anything we need at any time we want, I believe we may be tapping into something more than the collective consciousness of Jung in the archetypal sense, but that we may actually have the ability to tap into a genetic memory of all who have gone before us and all who will ever exist.

I believe using our sheer consciousness that we are able to tap into the minds of our ancestors as well as all of their hopes and dreams, realized or unrealized.

At night I often close my eyes and I am bombarded with strange images of people I have never seen before in places far away where I have never been. I feel my mind is like a transmitter on a radio and I am tuned into some very strange stations, picking up all sorts of things.

One particular instance that is very fresh in my mind happened when I went to Cairo, Egypt for the first time. After spending so much time on the plane, I was exhausted when I arrived there and that first night I began to see people in my mind, moaning as if they were starving and suffering tremendously. It was almost more than I could stand. I woke up in the night and told my friend I was not able to sleep, I felt I was picking up on age old suffering of many generations there.

The next day after having an amazing tour of the city and pyramids, I asked that this information stay out of my mind so I could sleep and by the third day I was fine again and ready to enjoy the trip.

This brings to mind the question I have been asking throughout this work – are we actually capable of not only feeling the feelings of our own ancestors who have come before us, but of becoming other people who we are not related to? I think the answer to that is yes, and if we can more consciously tap into that space of learning the things that others who have come before already knew, we would shorten our own learning curves and there is no telling what we could create.

I have previously mentioned in my book *Lifestream* the Greek concept of the 'river of forgetfulness.' This is the idea that when we are born, we make a pact with the higher power to dive into a river upon our birth and when we dive in, we forget all our souls have ever known so we can come here and have a richer experience. The ideal is that when we come into every incarnation we are a *tabula rasa*, or blank slate, ready to learn everything, including our own soul chosen lessons in life, as if our souls chose what we are to experience here before we arrived.

Occasionally I encounter case histories of people who claim they chose not to dip into that forgetful space and so they were born totally aware and more conscious than others and found the experience to be quite boring. Whether that is true or it is merely a function of an over-inflated ego is not for me to judge, but what I do believe is that in our forgetful state, if we understand that we can tap into higher intelligence, there are many amazing things we could accomplish to forward humanity to a place of great peace and prosperity.

Certainly that is the function of history, to read about those who have come before so we may either gain from their experience or attempt to avoid costly mistakes. What I am talking about here is a step beyond that – actually tapping into the minds of the great ones themselves so we can better mankind.

What if I can talk to Einstein, Newton or Galileo myself instead of just reading about them? Psychics and intuitives claim to channel various entities and energies with this concept in mind. I believe without going into the mind reading business we can all tap into this storehouse of information.

Forty Two
Hundredth Monkey

This is one of my favorite stories to relay to my students and to ponder when thinking about how we're all so connected to one another.

There is an old study first described by Lyall Watson and later by Ken Keyes in the book *Hundredth Monkey* about some monkeys who learned to wash sand off of potatoes so they would taste better.

The first monkey to wash the potato shared the trick with her mother and soon many monkeys were able to make them taste better, but it was not until 100 monkeys learned the secret that the knowledge spread rapidly throughout the island where they lived.

It was suggested that once the consciousness reaches a certain level then it shifts, and in this case, monkeys all over the world were able to wash their food.

The same justification is used in transcendental Meditation movement. It is thought that if enough people meditate at once, the consciousness of the planet will shift and peace will abound.

Because this happened, it suggests there may be some kind of energetic field, or frequency, that we all have access to and that when enough of us access information, it becomes readily available to us all.

It reminds me of when I first wrote and completed the prequel to this book, *Beyond Reality: Evidence of Parallel Universes*, in the fall of 2003.

I was excited and couldn't wait to put it out there, yet my intuition told me to wait. My intuition told me that the concepts would not be accepted as well as if I waited until a later time.

I forgot all about it until I was in Sedona, Arizona, in the summer of 2004 giving some talks when a friend and I went to see the wonderful new, at the time, film called *What the Bleep Do We Know?!?* After seeing it, I instantly knew it was time to put my ideas forth.

The film was created in the Northwest and one of the first places it was shown nationally was Sedona. I knew it would be slowly creeping about the states and as it did, my work could be more accepted.

I mentioned *Bleep* earlier in the book, ad if you saw it, you know that in the film, actress Marlee Matlin takes a journey through quantum reality and we see with great visual clarity how every step she takes and every thought she has creates her reality.

In one scene she tells herself "I hate you!" and we see her warp into an ugly mess, while later she says "I love you!" and we see her turn back into her same beautiful self.

What later occurred to me is that while I was busy typing away at *Beyond Reality*, the filmmakers were working on *What the Bleep*. It's as if there was some common thought form floating around in the atmosphere and people were tuning in to it all at once.

By 2005, the ideas about parallel universes were widely known, due to the film and book *Elegant Universe*, and others that hit the main stream audience.

It reminds me of the phenomenon when great inventions are made and several different people rush to the patent office at the same time.

The patent invariably goes to the first person to arrive, but what this suggests is that something much bigger than ourselves is at play.

To me, it is evidence that we must all be connected somehow to a greater intelligence and that we are all tuning into the same information simultaneously.

In the case of my research, I felt it was validating on many levels, and the more people begin to talk about this phenomenon, the more we can all learn to accept these extremely complex concepts as reality and shift our consciousness.

The idea of the hundred monkeys is exciting to leaders in our world today who hope that by illustrating this example we can show people how simple it would be to live in and create a more peaceful world.

It doesn't take much - just a change of thinking, is all - to affect a profound change in our world.

You may think you are only one little, insignificant person out there and wonder what you can possibly do to influence the world around you, yet it is absolute fact that you are helping to create our world by your very existence.

These really are profound times.

Forty Three
Lemarck's Moths:
Living Evolution

In the early stages of evolution theories, 19th century theorist Jean Baptist Lemarck developed a theory that certain traits were passed down from generation to generation, at least in part due to environmental factors.

One example sited were giraffes, which Lemarck believed needed longer and longer necks to reach leaves and therefore passed those traits on to offspring.

In his other major study, he studied moths near Manchester, England. Some moths were pure white, some pure black and because the houses were white, initially the white moths were able to survive longer because of their camouflage while the black ones were being eaten by birds and were near extinction.

When the industrial revolution started, soot and other pollutants filled the air and colored the rooftops of houses with soot. Nearly overnight the black moths began to make a comeback and bred with some of the white moths, creating a new speckled variety, while the white moths nearly died out.

The point of the theory, again, is that the environment, or external factors contributed to the evolution of the species and this was not due solely to heredity.

It is my experience that evolution is happening at every moment we are alive and we, like the pepper-colored moths, are adapting to a fast paced society and all the many changes that surround us all the time, even on a daily or hourly basis.

You are who you are right now because of your genetics. You were born into this life with certain traits and features and ways of being that were passed to you from your ancestral heritage.

Then there's the factors psychologists call nurture. This refers to how your parents treated you, what they taught you and how you were affected by those around you – your friends, teachers, and acquaintances.

Beyond that, you are also affected by the books you read, TV shows and movies you watch and people you choose to spend your time with. I once worked for a motivational speaker who said you can never underestimate the power of influence and asked everyone to take a mental stock of who they were around.

Every minute of every day, particularly in this computer-aged society, you are bombarded with all kinds of information and how you interpret that is based on every single thing you've ever thought, done, said, or experienced before. It's like going through life and looking at it through your own unique set of 'you' glasses. There is nobody like you. Nobody at all, and yet the sum total of who you are, is made up of so many things that came before you.

In the invisible realm of consciousness there is an energetic field that we all are a part of, and although we can't quite see it, it is making you who you are and affecting every single thing about your life.

Connected to that field is everyone and everything else in the entire universe. If you can take time to realize and become more aware of that connection you have with all the other stuff out there, you will begin to notice there are ways to just know things that were previously not a part of your personal experience. It's like waking up from a dream and seeing things and how they are really all connected to each other.

When you change a feeling or thought or heal something from your past, everything else in this field becomes more peaceful and more relaxed because of your choice. As more and more of these feelings become more peaceful from more and more people, all things become possible.

Whatever you want to choose to experience in your life is up to you depending on what part of this field you want to tune into, just like you choose which radio station to listen to and what kind of music you want to hear. Don't like what life is giving you? Fine, just turn the channel and go someplace else. You can do this right now just by changing what you focus on and what you're thinking about things.

All of your wildest dreams are sitting there dormant in the unified field of possibility, just waiting for your time and your attention. Go there now and see what's in store for you and I know you can live out your wildest dreams

Beyond Reality
Conclusion

I had a heated discussion recently with a colleague about the source of ideas. As a science fiction writer, he said he knows his ideas come from him and are completely original. I disagreed with this and I wish you could've seen the look on his face when I did.

I do not believe in completely original thought. Sure, we all have moments of inspiration, but even in our most creative moments I believe we are tapping into a higher power or a higher source.

Every time you read a book, watch a TV show or simply talk to a neighbor you are learning things, thinking about things and hopefully refining the way you view the world around you. It would be nearly impossible to do anything but that.

Of course, you hear about those who are so set in their ways they still have shag carpet in their houses and listen to eight tracks, but for the most part, we were designed to be fluid – an ever evolving species.

Within that flow of feeling thought and inspiration, you use your own unique filters to then go about the process of creating something 'new' from all of it. I would say your creation is uniquely you because only your filters at that moment in space-time could create exactly what you created at that moment.

Yet how could you create anything at all if your parents never taught you to speak, to feed and clothe yourself or to tie your shoes?

And what about all the influences you and I have had from so many sources? To me, we are all living evolution at ever moment of our existence.

We've talked repeatedly about the fact that no system can understand itself fully and I certainly think that is the case with mankind. Considering everything from which came first, chicken or egg, to whether or not the Big Bang was an actual event, in my mind, mankind will continue to struggle with the fundamental question I think perplexes us all: why are we here?

Most of us would like to think there is a source from which all things came and at some point there was a beginning and that unseen force began this crazy thing we call life.

Yet somehow these things seem to be so totally paradoxical it is tough to come to any definitive conclusions about how we arrived at this moment and where we started from. It is truly *Beyond Reality*.

There is an underlying web of consciousness I believe we all tap into at some level.

Every day, every thought we have begins in the unmanifest wave of this powerful field.

Our brains are like radio transmitters and you have the choice right now to create the life you want to live simply by tuning in to whatever it is you want to create.

The true nature of reality is in the eyes of whoever is experiencing it, so choose wisely, fellow traveler, and may your journey be as adventurous and exciting as your wildest dreams will allow.

Bibliography

Asimov, Isaac. *Foundation*. New York, NY: Bantam Books, 1991.

Asimov, Isaac. *Foundation & Empire*. New York, NY: Bantam Books, 1992.

Asimov, Isaac. *The Universe: From Flat Earth to Black Holes and Beyond.* New York, NY: Walker and Company, 1966.

Bristol, Claude M. *The Magic of Believing: The Science of Setting Your Goal...and then Reaching It!* New York, NY: Cornerstone Library, 1948.

Brown, Dan. *Angels & Demons.* New York, NY: Simon and Schuster, 2000.

Calaprice, Alice. *The Quotable Einstein.* Princeton, NJ: The Princeton University Press, 1996.

Carroll, Lee. *Kryon Book 9: The New Beginning.* Del Mar, CA: Hayhouse, 2002.

Chown, Marcus. *"The Black Hole Survival Guide: Falling into a black hole need not spell certain doom."* New *Scienti*st, September 6-12, 2003.

Davies, Paul. *The Cosmic Blueprint: New Discoveries in Nature's Creative Ability to Order the Universe.* New York, NY: Simon and Schuster, 1988.

Davies, Paul. *"How to Build a Time Machine: It wouldn't be easy, but it might be possible."* *Scientific American*, September 2002.

Dictionary.com "Channelling."

Eddington, Arthur. *Space, Time, and Gravitation: An Outline of the General Relativity Theory.* New York, NY: Cambridge University Press, 1920.

Fiore, Edith. *The Unquiet Dead: A Psychologist Treats Spirit Possession.* New York, NY: Ballantine Books, 1988.

Greene, Brian. *The Elegant Universe: Superstrings, Hidden Dimensions and the Quest for the Ultimate Theory.* New York, NY: WW Norton and Company, 1999.

Greene, Brian. *"The Future of String Theory –A Conversation with Brian Greene: The physicist and best-selling author demystifies the ultimate theories of space and time, the nature of genius, multiple universes, and more."* *Scientific American*, November 2003.

Gribbin, John. *Q is for Quantum: An Encyclopedia of Particle Physics.* New York, NY: The Free Press, 1998.

Hawking, Stephen. *A Brief History of Time: From the Big Bang to Black Holes.* New York, NY: Bantam Books, 1988.

Hawking, Stephen. *Universe in Nutshell.* New York: NY: Bantam Books, 2001.

Holt, Jim. *"My So Called Universe: Our Cozy World is probably much bigger – and stranger – than we know."* (MSN.com http://slate.msn.com/id/2087206/) August 20, 2003.

James Tad & Wyatt Woodsmall. *Timeline Therapy and the Basis of Personality.* Cupertino, CA: Meta Publications, 1988.

Johnson, George. *A Shortcut Through Time: The Path to the Quantum Computer.* New York: NY: Alfred A Knopf, 2003.

Kaku, Michio. *Hyperspace: A Scientific Odyssey Through Parallel Universes, Time Warps, and the 10th Dimension.* New York, NY: Simon & Schuster, 1994.

Keys, Ken, Jr. *The Hundredth Monkey.* Vision Books, 1982.

Lewis, C.S. *The Lion, the Witch and the Wardrobe.* New York, NY: Harper Collins, 1950.

Linewater, Charles H. *What is the Universe Made of? How Old Is It?* (Los Amalos National Laboratory Archives: http://xxx.lanl.gov/abs/astro-ph/9911294)

Maddox, Sire John. *"The Unexpected Science to Come...The most important discoveries of the next 50 years are likely to be ones of which we cannot now even conceive." Scientific American,* December 1999.

Montgomery, Ruth. *A World Beyond.* New York: NY: Fawcett Crest, 1971.

Minkel, JR. *"Borrowed Time: Interview with Michio Kaku: A theoretical physicist contemplates the plausibility of time travel."* Scientific American, November 2003.

New Scientist Magazine. *"Into the Black Hole,"* September 6-12, 2003.

Oxford Dictionary of Quotations. New York, NY: 1979.

Rees, Martin. *Just Six Numbers: The Deep Forces that Shape the Universe.* Great Britain: Basic Books, 1999.

Roberts, Jane. *Dreams, "Evolution," and Value Fulfillment Volume One: A Seth Book.* San Rafael, CA: Amber-Allen Publishing, 1986.

Shermer, Michael. *"Digits and Fidgets: Is the universe fine-tuned for life?"* Scientific American, January 2003.
Sitchin, Zecharia. *The 12th Planet: Book I of the Earth Chronicles.* New York, NY: Avon Books, 1976.

Smoot, George and Keay Davidson. *Wrinkles in Time.* New York: NY: William Morrow and Company, Inc., 1993.

Taylor, John. *When the Clock Struck Zero: Science's Ultimate Limits.* New York, NY: St. Martin's Press, 1993.

Tegmark, Max. *"Parallel Universes: Not Just a Staple of Science Fiction, other universes are a direct implication of cosmological observations."* Scientific American, April 2003.

Thorne, Kip S. *Black Holes and Time Warps: Einstein's Outrageous Legacy.* New York: WW Norton and Company, Inc., 1994.

Tsuchida, A. *"What exactly is Déjà vu?" Scientific American*, May 2002.

Wakefield, Julie. *"A Mind for Consciousness: Somewhere in the brain, Christof Koch believes, there are certain clusters of neurons that will explain why you're you and not someone else." Scientific American,* July 2001.

Walker, J.R. The Sun Dance and Other Ceremonies of the Oglala Division of the Teton Dakota (American Museum of Natural History, Anthropological Papers, vol XVI, part II, (1917) pp.152-3)

Wolf, Fred Alan. *Parallel Universes: The Search for Other Worlds.* New York, NY: Simon & Schuster, 1988.

Printed in the United States
69326LVS00001B/172